THE DOONESBURY CHRONICLES

Doonesbury Books in Holt Paperback Editions

THE DOONESBURY CHRONICLES
G. B. Trudeau
With an Introduction by Garry Wills

An Owl Book / Henry Holt and Company / New York

You could be laughing at me,
You've got the right.
But you go on smiling...
                    —Jackson Browne

Introduction by Garry Wills

Almost every one of us so-called adult male Americans is a jock manqué. We only decided to be above all that the time when it dawned on us we were just not good enough for the pros—or even for the midget team. (My own basketball was played on a humiliatingly submidget team called "The Mosquitos.") For a while, there was a consolation prize. Perhaps stardom was out of reach; but one might still become the obviously next-best-thing, a sports *announcer*. In fact, we had already been that in all our daydreaming of stardom. What good is it to knock out a ghostly home run, or dunk a phantom basketball, if the world does not hear of it and shout approval? So watch boys dribbling on a downtown asphalt court or cuffing balls across a sandlot—you will, in time, trace an odd antiphonal pattern of sportscasters "announcing" each boy's game. "Here comes Denny the Dunk up the court, making fantastic moves," Denny reports to the tiered thousands of invisible Denny-fans.

And Lenny, covering him, has his own announcer: "But Slick Lenny has him all sewed up—and almost steals the ball! What hands!" Almost every boy who ever dabbled in sports has spent hours being three things all at once—performer, announcer, and fan. It is one of the basic exercises in that shared human trait of watching, judging, and approving (or groaning at) one's own activity. Chesterton once said that we are the only laboratory specimens that study themselves through a microscope that *is* ourselves.

In 1968 the Yale *Daily News* featured a cartoon strip by an undergraduate named Garry Trudeau. The Yale football team's star quarterback at the time was Brian Dowling, and one way to deflate the superstar back to the general level of us duffers and misfits was to imagine him still doing the internal patter of adulation long after he had acquired a real announcer to celebrate his feats. So there goes big Number Ten, "B.D.," into the huddle—he calls the play as if he were announcing it during the execution: "I fade back to our own five-yard line. Waiting until at least three men are upon me, balancing on one foot, I throw an underhand ninety-five-yard spiral, which I'll run down and catch on the goal line."

But it is even more satisfying to imagine the great B.D. off the field, announcing other kinds of games that all men play. Here he is at a college mixer, beginning to socialize: "While he coolly sips on his ginger ale, the young college quarterback awaits the rush which will undoubtedly come when word gets out that he is here at Briarcliff . . . ." And, just in case they don't recognize him, B.D. is still wearing his football helmet. (Later, of course, B.D. the all-American jock will go to Vietnam and wear that same helmet instead of the military kind—the white Yale helmet even gets autographed by Bob Hope after one of his Christmas shows.)

If it is fun to dream of a successful jock still dreaming of becoming a successful jock, it is even better to watch B.D.'s klutzy roommate, Mike Doonesbury, "announcing" his miserable performances: "Mike 'the Mix,' inexperienced but eager freshman, still looks around for his first score of the evening"—only to be addressed finally as "you gross, skinny frosh." Always, of course, Trudeau's characters give themselves their own sports nicknames, which tend to become ludicrous in other people's mouths. Doonesbury cheers himself on as "Mike the Mix" and "Mike the Man." Mark Slackmeyer, campus radical, comes before us to seize the university president's home: "With discontent in the air, the SDS has staged a rally in front of the president's house, led by 'Megaphone' Mark." Unfortunately for the Megaphone, others reduce him to scale by using the silly diminutive "Megs." You can't win if you're a Trudeau character.

Even the president of Yale, Kingman Brewster, plays sports announcer to his own performance in the campus wars: "It's more kudos for Yale's Youthful President as he starts out on his morning walk through the colleges to reduce tension." But while he preens himself abroad, Slackmeyer has seized his home.

Jim Andrews, of the Universal Press Syndicate, found Trudeau's strip in the *Daily News* and asked to syndicate it commercially. He was repaid, later in their friendship, by entering the strip as an oil magnate during the 1974 gasoline shortage. At first Trudeau just slightly recast his old situations to fit every campus and the family newspapers: The "Y" got scrubbed off B.D.'s helmet, naked girls in the dorms got their clothes put back on, and swear words disappeared. But Trudeau's world opened up when he got into the realm of politics. Despite Megaphone Mark's rallies, and Mike's inept drags on a marijuana joint, there had been only one strip of real political satire in the Yale days—when B.D. so cowed and abused his replacement in a huddle that the rest of the team called the underdog "Hubert."

All that changed in the extraordinarily successful commercial strips from which this book is assembled: B.D. went to war, and Mike started tutoring in the ghetto, and Joanie Caucus ran away from her husband and children to be liberated. Mark even dragged Mike off to a peace march in Washington, where Mike argued with Joe Alsop while Mark called on Vice-President Humphrey (heard still trying to spell his name over the phone to President Nixon).

Yet the world that Trudeau entered remained close to his basic insight. Send B.D. to Vietnam, where he gets captured, and his captor will introduce himself to an inaudible ringside cheer: "Who ain't heard of Phred the Terrorist?" Phred, it turns out, is just joining the family business—his father pressured him into the firm. Zonker Harris, the flowery freak-out who tends Walden Puddle, goes to Vietnam to cover B.D.'s exploits in sportscasts from the front. The coffee-house priest introduces himself in the third person, and with reference to his clips: "The fighting young priest who can talk to the young . . . Birmingham, Selma, Chicago '68." A ghetto tour is conducted as if for television. Jeb Magruder's penitence becomes an "In Concert" traveling show. Everything is "covered" as a sports event.

During the Senate Watergate hearings, Megaphone Mark took a job as a disc jockey and became "Marvelous Mark," playing Watergate profiles as personal-request numbers: "Okay! Profile on John Dean III going out to Joey with hugs from Donna!" When Trudeau had Mark conclude his judicious profile on John Mitchell by doing an ecstatic jig to cries of "Guilty, guilty, guilty!" the Washington *Post* killed the strip and editorialized: "We cannot have one standard for the news pages and another for the comics." I agree. How can the rest of us journalists ever live up to Trudeau's standards?

The sportscaster technique even served Trudeau in the least likely connection—his affectionate portrait of the "libber" Joanie Caucus. Billie Jean King helped, of course. Ms. Caucus and women's sports arrived simultaneously in the day-care center: "We can't *all* wear tennis dresses with blue sequins. Basically, it's just not possible. Anyway, I'm thinking of changing to Margaret Mead." That last sentence shows us why the self-announcing trait of Trudeau's characters is not limited to males or to jocks. Joanie's day-care children are only liberated by taking on role-models—"B.J." King, or Ms. Mead, or Joanie herself. And even Joanie can only break the mold of what she is "supposed" to be by taking up a publicly defined role—"women's libber," a type delivered to her in the newspapers. She is testing her "game" against Betty Friedan's, as surely as the sandlot kid is re-enacting a Ted Williams performance.

Trudeau's way of making characters deliver a running commentary on their own acts, a commentary cast in the third person, opens up that inner space in which personality can grow. We think too often of "playing a role" as something artificial, at odds with reality. But we are all role-players, to our roots. We become by pretending. We feign humanity. We must "play" child before we get a chance to "play" adult—and in both cases we are quietly watching and indulgently grading (even while fearing or resenting) our own performance. The process of growth is in large part a willingness to risk new roles—something Joanie perfectly exemplifies in her breakout. She runs away on Mark's motorbike long after she should have "settled down" in her one role as wife-mother. B.D. kids Mike when the cyclists arrive back at the commune with Joanie: "Little of the ol' Mrs. Robinson, eh, Mikey?" But Joanie, getting on toward Mrs. Robinson's age, is more like the kids in *The Graduate*. Except that her breakout is both more difficult and more realistic—she is rushing off to find a job, not to escape one. In fact, eventually she will be "A Graduate"—a new role for her—if Berkeley's law school survives her incursion. And meanwhile she teaches not only her day-care charges, but her young friends in the commune as well.

Humor is always complex and precarious—the Real's nervous *j'accuse* hurled at the Ideal, in the name of the Ideal. That is why the humor that ultimately fails is the kind that does not take itself seriously enough—without the risk, there is no joke. And a humor that has Trudeau's starting point makes its own complexity the point. Mike at the mixer *is* what he bills himself as: "Inexperienced but eager freshman" looking around for his first score. But that hardly makes him "Mike the Mix." Still, he must try to be Mike the Mix in order to stand his ground at all, to keep from running away. We all only pretend to be heroes—even our heroes. (That is what B.D. is all about.)

Trudeau's characters are watching each other watch themselves, just like the rest of us. We travel toward ourselves by detours only. We grow not so much by addition as by division—and multiplication. The more "things" we are, the more roles we have tried, the more we become a unique and united self. The "simple" man is less than a man, and much of a corpse. The complex man is an army on the move. That is why Trudeau's kind of talking-to-oneself is the only way, finally, to communicate with others.

Trudeau's approach has a very practical effect on his strip. Since his characters are caught in the process of defining themselves over-against some public role, they have no trouble moving out, anywhere, into the world. Mark can as easily talk to Hubert Humphrey as to Brian Dowling or to "King" Brewster. That is not as common an ability as one might think in today's "funnies," which have by and large tended a small "lyrical" garden and an inner world. "Peanuts" is as good an example as any: Its world is a playground uncontaminated by adults, or even by the clothes, furniture, or reminders of adults. The strip says that we are all children; there are no adults. That view has just enough truth in it to get by, but the strip does so by a drastic narrowing. The fantasy-for-its-own-sake ends up logically in a dog's dream of being a German air-ace. This is not role-playing as a way of trying on a world to see if it fits, but as a way of escaping the world. Happiness is a toy puppy's nose. Much the same thing can be said of Broom Hilda's blasted heath, or Pogo's later (desiccating) swamp. Al Capp kept his strip alive so long because Abner could leave Dogpatch and go to Washington, or to Lower Slobbovia. When Walt Kelly dragged Joe McCarthy and Spiro Agnew into the swamp, that upset its ecology forever. The more interesting characters, like Miz Mam'selle Hepzibah and Porky Pine, began to lose their particular reality.

The natural terminus of this shrinking "inner world" of comedy is the solipsism of Jules Feiffer's characters, who pursue themselves expressionlessly through panel after panel and crumble when they catch themselves. Trudeau has obviously learned from Feiffer; he uses repeated panels with little or no visual change to indicate thought processes going on *behind* a façade. But Feiffer's characters are stranded in a desert of themselves, while Trudeau's people interact. Indeed, it is when he is superficially most like Feiffer that the difference becomes clearest.

Richard Nixon is a voice coming out of the TV set, that just sits there for panel after panel. Then, at the end, even klutzy Mike Doonesbury's head drops in embarrassment for the overreacher's last mendacity. The "Nixon" portrayed here—or, rather, studiously left unportrayed—is not the historian's Nixon, or the journalist's. He is the Nixon whose voice enters Walden Puddle's commune and makes its residents react. He is the Nixon B.D. praises when others wonder how the man kept a silly war going so long: "The President is a lot smarter than you think."

So Trudeau, despite his sketchy and Feifferesque economy of drawing, has brought narrative back to the *funny* strips (as opposed to inked-in soap operas), where it has been missing since the great days of Capp's schmoos and kygmies. B.D.'s capture by Phred gave Trudeau a way to arch a single story over several weeks while keeping each segment funny. And we have to keep reminding ourselves of the truly astonishing achievement this represents—that he made us laugh at the Vietnam war during its most corrosive stages. Trudeau's Vietnam was, to the late sixties, what Capp's Slobbovia was to the Cold-War forties.

Yet the war strips in Vietnam were not the toughest challenge Trudeau set for himself. For that prize I would nominate the tour de force of Phred's visit to Washington, accompanied by three hundred refugees disguised as Coca-Cola (*they're the real thing*). You have to remember the story (a sign of the characters' strength): Phred, to keep the sports-star analogy alive, was up for renewal of his terrorist contract; but he was asking too much—his mother wanted a fresh motorbike for her *plastiqueuse* getaways. So Phred gets traded to another team (the Pathet Lao). After tiring of the scenery in Laos (mainly refugees as far as the eye can see), he took a tourist flight to beautiful Cambodia, where most of the briefly remaining scenery was also refugees. He asked an oriental Grant Wood couple (complete with pitchfork) if their museum was destroyed in the secret Cambodian bombings:

"*Secret* bombings? . . . I remarked on them. I said, 'Look, Martha, here come the bombs.'"

"It's true, he did."

That set up the situation. Then Trudeau launched four weeks of strips that brought homeless refugees to Washington as congressional witnesses. (They fly in on a plane returning empty Coke bottles to keep a ruined Cambodia beautiful.) Hunger and tragedy yield a weird music of laughter. The hearings, needless to say by now, get "announced" as a quiz show: Who can identify a phantom jet while being bombed by it? What *prizes* for the witnesses? Mike watches the hearings at home. Though he is B.D.'s old roommate, he has not (yet) met Phred. It is a large world Trudeau has taken to roaming in; and only we, the readers, are let into all parts of it.

It is surprising that politics freed Trudeau for these wanderings. The political animals that entered Okefenokee contaminated it, and the later humor of "Li'l Abner" crumpled under a kind of political hatred. Capp's Joanie Phoney was not only less fair than Joanie Caucus, from a political point of view, she was just less funny. Ms. Caucus is not an anti-Phoney. The reason is, again, Trudeau's creative interplay of the self against its roles. Though the satire has bite, it remains surprisingly kindly. There are no really hateful characters in the strip—not even the pilots who casually erase entire countries under their wing-tips while discussing a Knicks game. Mark, the radical, is not hated—and neither are the hard hats who beat him up. Some might consider Phred the acid test—what other artist could make a terrorist amiable? Not even the Watergate criminals were treated with unbridled bitterness. Not even Nixon, who was presented as a kind of Dagwood under his various imperial roles; all the evil demands he made upon himself and could not, mercifully, meet. The most moving cartoon on the President's resignation showed the demolition of a brick wall that grew up around the White House in earlier strips. It seemed more like the freeing of a prisoner than the storming of a bastille.

Over and over Trudeau affects a neat, almost surgical division between indignation and malice. Usually only sanctity can make such hairline incisions; but comedy, too, is a thing of rigor and discipline, a kind of secular asceticism (ask the best of them, Mark Twain). Trudeau's characters fail and bumble themselves into our affection. It is one thing to laugh at a klutz; it is another thing entirely to laugh at a man who is obviously mocking himself for being a klutz. He has co-opted us, this Doonesbury. We laugh with him, in a camaraderie of klutziness. "Mike the Man" is silly. But ridicule only deflates him to "Mike, a Man"—and there is no higher earthly title. Trudeau always sees a person *under* the roles, struggling with them. His wisdom mocks forgivingly, and each target of his ridicule is haloed with laughter's benediction.

Author's Preface:

Four years four months gone by, and I find myself ready to embark on what is shaping up to be an arduous fact-finding mission to Pago Pago, which is, at least this year, the seat of government in American Samoa. Yes, it has come to that. In the event that for one reason or another I don't survive the crossing of the international date line, I must make my peace and leave behind these cryptic notes, with the hope that they will ultimately find their way into the comprehensive retrospective now in the making.

I have just finished reading an astonishingly well-reasoned critique of "Doonesbury," written and sent to me by Alice, age eight, president of a Tallahassee chapter of the Sunshine and Smiles John Denver Fan Club. The letter is filled with angry words for me, for I have slighted her idol in some recent strips, and, as I have learned this past month, hell hath no fury like that of a fan of John Denver scorned. Nonetheless, for all its excesses, the letter seems to me particularly forthright, written with an urgency and directness that invariably characterize the communications of the very young. Walt Kelly, creator of "Pogo," used to believe that cartoonists should be attended at all times by staffs of small, insouciant children in whose wisdom and vision he correctly placed absolute faith. To see through the essentially egalitarian eyes of a child, where nothing escapes notice and everything starts out with an equal importance, is to celebrate the boundless, shimmering diversity of everyday experience. The young seem to reach out to grasp *all* of life's perceptual confetti: colors and cues, sights and sounds, notions of every sort are permitted wondrous entry. Nothing is ignored and nothing is wasted. With wobbly logic and earnest assumptions, children are free to order their priorities more or less randomly; only later are they taught that the blackboard is more important than the wall that frames it.

The rest of us can only envy from afar this tumbled but guileless universe. As the naturalist Annie Dilliard lamented, "I would like to know grasses and sedges—and *care*. Then my least journey into the world would be a series of happy recognitions." And happy recognitions, no matter how seemingly common, are the stuff from which the dreams and fantasies of children are conjured. Nothing else is required. In the quintessential cartoon fantasy of Slumberland in Winsor McCay's "Little Nemo," a small boy dropped off to sleep and the tiniest objects of his day were transformed into the wondrous vehicles of his nights. In his dreams, Nemo floated on a milkweed seed, toppled from a colossal mushroom, and was whisked away in an ivory coach drawn by cream-colored rabbits. The scale of the objects corresponded to the importance that the boy attached to them—hence, giant raspberries and miniature furniture. Through it all, the value of

Slumberland established itself through its contribution to the child's experience, and when the excitement of the vision deposited him, as it always did, in a jumble of sheets on the hardwood floor beside his bed, it was only the artist's implicit assurance that Nemo would have other dreams to explore that kept away the disappointment.

A flight of fantasy, whether in dream or daydream, is no mere sleight of mind. But only children will accept it as being equally as profound as the arbitrary state of awareness we are taught to regard as reality, and hence, only they are nurtured by it. Later, of course, many of us comprehend our self-imposed poverty and try to double back, but the bread crumbs are always missing and our failures are immense. A true belief in the validity of nonordinary reality—with all that it can teach us—seems beyond the capabilities of every practicing adult, with the possible exception of Federico Fellini.

Perhaps this sad state of affairs helps explain the indispensable function of the cartoonist in society. When he's doing his job, he provides us with the means to look back into ourselves; he's the benign conduit between our self-serious façades and those pockets of vulnerability buried deep within. The challenges he negotiates are considerable: to create a compelling fantasy—whether Slumberland or Okefenokee—and to invite the reader to involve himself in a new reality set up as a sustained metaphor for his own; to let the small meannesses and foolishnesses of life face each other in distortion, stretched, juggled, and juxtaposed, but always lit with laughter to ease the pain of self-recognition; to seek out the vignette that speaks much to the lives of many; to distill and refine language so as to epitomize, and to look everywhere for simple meanings—even in the grasses and sedges. These are the purposes of the precious few in this business who have really meant something to their readers; the purposes of artists who had the capability of endowing a given strip with such exquisite flow of allusion that one almost expected it to lift like a decal and float off the page.

As many of the cartoons in this collection amply demonstrate, there are myriad places to go wrong. In what is unavoidably a chronicle of one's own personal maturation, self-indulgence and contrivance abound. And in the pursuit of tomfoolery the desire to join battle sometimes overwhelms. Yet, in more thoughtful moments, I have tried to observe Kelly's famous advice of almost twenty years ago: "There is no need to sally forth, for it remains true that those things which make us human are, curiously enough, always close at hand. Resolve, then, that on this very ground, with small flags waving, and tiny blasts of tinny trumpets, we have met the enemy, and not only may he be ours, he may be us."

Garry Trudeau
New Haven, Connecticut
February 26, 1975

I/High Tides and Greener Grass

It wasn't just Mark Slackmeyer on a proletariat lark, taking a hard-hat job over summer vacation—*everybody* was just dying to establish a dialogue. If you were a college professor, it might help to bring in for your class an actual Black Panther, or offer a course in Consciousness 10-A. Even better if you were a fighting young priest who could talk to the young. Still, communications could be requited, or unrequited, on more fundamental planes: Doonesbury working on his timing at fraternity mixers, Mark's father trying to tune in on his son via "Mod Squad," and B.D. turning from the frustrations of the huddle to the invigorating, simpler pleasures of combat training. Everything, if not everyone, seemed poised.

MR. PRESIDENT, I ASSUME YOU ARE AWARE OF THE RALLY, WE HAVE PLANNED FOR NEXT SATURDAY..

YES, CALVIN?

I HAVE HERE A STATEMENT EXPRESSING YOUR SKEPTICISM THAT A BLACK REVOLUTIONARY CAN GET A FAIR TRIAL..

IF YOU SIGN IT, I CAN GUARANTEE NO VIOLENCE THIS WEEKEND, THEREBY MAKING YOU A NATIONAL FOLK-HERO FOR KEEPING THE PEACE.

RIGHT ON.

IN CONCLUDING MY REMARKS, I WOULD LIKE TO COMMENT ON THE PANTHER TRIAL...

PERSONALLY, I AM SKEPTICAL OF THE ABILITY OF A BLACK REVOLUTIONARY TO GET A FAIR TRIAL IN THE UNITED STATES...

THANK YOU AND GOOD NIGHT.

THE BALL'S IN YOUR COURT, SPIRO.

MR. PRESIDENT, I JUST WANTED TO THANK YOU FOR BEING SO HELPFUL WITH OUR RALLY.... IT WAS A BIG SUCCESS

FOR ONE DAY, WE WERE ALL BROTHERS, FIGHTING FOR SOMETHING STRONG AND MARVELOUS. IT WAS A BEAUTIFUL EXPERIENCE.

RIGHT. NOW GET OUT.

SO MUCH FOR CAMELOT.

HEY, CALVIN, WHY SO GLUM?

WELL, MARK, NOW THAT THE RALLY'S OVER, I FEEL A TREMENDOUS VOID. IT'S AS IF WE REVOLUTIONARY BLACKS HAVE NO PLACE TO GO...

SIGH...

EVER THOUGHT OF BECOMING A CIVIL RIGHTS NEGRO?

MRS. JACKSON? I'M MICHAEL DOONESBURY, RUFUS'S NEW TUTOR..

OH, YES, COME IN.

I WAS KIND OF HOPING THE UNIVERSITY WOULD SEND A BLACK STUDENT. RUFUS'S LAST WHITE TUTOR ONLY LASTED A WEEK.

RUFUS, THIS IS MICHAEL DOONESBURY. I HOPE YOU'LL MAKE HIM FEEL RIGHT AT HOME.

WELCOME, YOU DUMB HONKY.

WELL, RUFUS, I HOPE THIS IS THE BEGINNING OF A REWARDING TEACHER-STUDENT RELATIONSHIP.. FAT CHANCE!

YOU DON'T FOOL ME, DOONESBURY! YOU'RE HERE BECAUSE YOU THINK YOU'RE TOUCHING ON THE BLACK EXPERIENCE! IN ADDITION, YOU STRIVE TO RELIEVE YOUR GUILT FEELINGS!

NONSENSE! I DON'T COME HERE TO RELIEVE MY GUILT FEELINGS!

THEN WHY MAN? WHY DO YOU COME DOWN HERE?

I'M PAID.

"SEE SPOT, RUN, DICK, WATCH HIM..."

HI, RUFUS, YOU BUSY, BABY?

HI, DIANE! DIANE, THIS IS MIKE, MY TUTOR. MIKE, MEET DIANE, MY WOMAN.

UH, HELLO..

HEY, DOLL-FACE, I'M INTO SOME HEAVY READING.. CATCH YOU LATER ON, O.K., BABY?

O.K., RUFUS HONEY.

"GO, JANE. GO SEE SPOT JUMP."

MOM! DAD! I'M HOME!

SO, SON, HOME FROM COLLEGE, ARE YOU?

WELCOME HOME, DEAR.

O.K., SON, LAY IT ON ME. TELL ME WHERE YOUR HEAD'S AT, AND MAYBE WE CAN GET IT TOGETHER. LIKE, LET'S GENERATE SOME GOOD VIBES.

WOW! HEAVY! DIG IT!

HE'S BEEN WATCHING "MOD SQUAD."

DEAR, I THINK IT'S ABOUT TIME YOU GOT DOWN TO BRASS TACKS AND FOUND A JOB.

YOU CAN'T SPEND YOUR WHOLE LIFE DRINKING BEER IN FRONT OF A T.V. SET.

WHAT ABOUT B.D.? DO YOU WANT YOUR ONLY SON TO THINK THAT HIS FATHER IS A QUITTER AND A LOSER?

FORTUNATELY, I'M TOO DRUNK TO ANSWER THAT QUESTION.

Dear Mr. President: I am writing in protest of my father being laid off at work. He only stays alive by being a janitor nights.

Last spring you said there is just as much dignity in being a janitor as in being President of the United States.

Right.

SOMETIMES A MAN HAS TO RESORT TO SARCASM..

MARIA, A RASH OF NEW BILLS CAME IN TODAY. $650. WORTH!

OH, DEAR, HOW COULD THINGS GET ANY WORSE FOR US?

GOOD AFTERNOON. I'M HERE TO RECLAIM YOUR TELEVISION.

MARIA, REFRESH MY MEMORY..

WHY EXACTLY DID WE LEAVE POLAND?

Dear Sir: Thank you for your recent letter. It moved me deeply.

As President of the United States, I find I usually don't have time to personally answer all my mail.

But your letter conveyed to me a personal problem that I don't hear too much about.

I was greatly saddened to hear that your ~~father~~ was laid off from his job at _the aircraft factory_.

..OOH! AREN'T YOU PROFESSOR GREEN?!

I'VE BEEN DYING TO MEET YOU!! I LOVED YOUR CUTE BOOK!

EVERYONE LOVES IT! DO YOU KNOW WHERE YOUR DARLING BOOK IS ALWAYS A BIG HIT?!.

COCKTAIL PARTIES!

HEY, MARK, I'D LIKE YOU TO MEET SOMEONE... THIS IS THE GUY WHO'S STARTED THIS NEW COFFEEHOUSE

ER, HI.

REVEREND SCOT SLOAN'S THE NAME, SON! I'M THE FIGHTING YOUNG PRIEST WHO CAN TALK TO THE YOUNG.

FIGHTING YOUNG PRIEST?

SURE, MAN. DIDN'T YOU READ ABOUT ME IN "LOOK"? BIRMINGHAM, SELMA, CHICAGO '68, WASHINGTON '67...?

OH, THAT FIGHTING YOUNG PRIEST.

RIGHT. NOW, CAN I LAY SOME JAVA ON YOU?

MICHAEL, FROM THE LOOKS OF THINGS SO FAR, I THINK MY COFFEEHOUSE HERE IS GOING TO CATCH, IT'S GOING TO GO!

IT'S JUST A HUNCH, SEE, BUT I CAN'T HELP FEELING YOU YOUTHS NEED SOMEPLACE TO COME WHEN YOU FEEL LIKE RELAXING. THIS COFFEE-HOUSE CAN BE THE PERFECT MILIEU. DYNAMIC, EXCITING, NOW.

..AND THE GOOD LORD WILLING, PERHAPS IT WILL EVEN TURN A PROFIT...

WHAT ARE YOU GOING TO USE THE PROFITS FOR?

TO WIPE OUT POVERTY, HUNGER, HATE, WAR, FRUSTRATION AND INADEQUATE HOUSING.

OH.

GOOD MORNING, BROTHER! WELCOME TO "THE EXIT," THE COFFEEHOUSE WHERE PEOPLE CAN REALLY RELATE!

REVEREND SCOT SLOAN'S THE NAME. PERHAPS YOU READ ABOUT ME IN "LOOK." I'M THE FIGHTING YOUNG PRIEST WHO CAN TALK TO THE YOUNG.

MY SPECIALTY, OF COURSE, IS SETTING UP DIALOGUES. OFTEN I AM SUCCESSFUL IN GETTING PEOPLE TO LOOK AT THEMSELVES HONESTLY AND MEANINGFULLY.

GOOD FOR YOU, SWEETHEART. ONE BLACK COFFEE TO GO.

II/The Sounds of Falling Dominoes

There was—had been, would be—a war. "To the 'Nam," B.D. called to his MATS pilot, and indeed there was a certain piquancy to life at Firebase Bundy, though it hardly prepared one for the likes of a Vietcong terrorist named Phred. On the home front a farmer could warble ". . . sweet land of subsidy," and the more callow slackards could huddle in communes. Some, like Zonker, could fall in love with a wheat patch. But the country out there, however schizophrenic, was too big to be ignored, at least so Mike and Mark must have reasoned before setting out on a transcontinental fact-finding motorcycle tour, an odyssey that netted them one runaway housewife. And if Joanie Caucus could turn her life around, so could . . . Zonker get a job as a mailman, the Reverend Scot Sloan go dating, and hard-headed B.D. see what the war was all about in stunned reunion with his pal the terrorist. Lines of sight were adjusting.

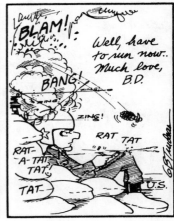

"DEAR GUYS, WELL, HERE I AM IN VIETNAM, AND BELIEVE ME, IT'S NO PICNIC!"

"THIS IS A DIRTY, ROTTEN, STINKING WAR, BUT I LOVE IT! EVEN STILL, I SPEND EVERY NIGHT IN FEAR, NOT KNOWING IF IT WILL BE MY LAST.."

MAN, IT GIVES ME SHIVERS READING THIS LETTER, MARK. JUST THINK OF THE ADVENTURES OL' B.D. MUST BE EXPERIENCING RIGHT NOW..

GIN! NUTS..

B.D.! GEORGE! GEORGE?

B.D., WE'VE BEEN LOOKING FOR YOU FOR A WEEK! I GOT LOST ON PATROL, GEORGE. LUCKILY, I MET PHRED HERE, WHO IS A V.C. TERRORIST, AND HE SAVED US BY FINDING A CACHE OF SCHLITZ! HIC

NOW LET ME GET THIS STRAIGHT... HIC

WOW! LOOK, GEORGE! IT'S A SCORE OF PHANTOM JETS OFF ON A PROTECTIVE REACTION RAID!

MAN, JUST LOOK AT THEM SCREAM ACROSS THE SKY! WHAT COULD BE MORE DELICATE AND BEAUTIFUL IN FLIGHT THAN A PHANTOM JET?

BRAVO FOR LIFE'S LITTLE IRONIES.

B.D...I CAN'T UNDERSTAND HOW YOU OF ALL PEOPLE BECAME FRIENDS WITH PHRED! I THOUGHT YOU HATED COMMUNISTS.

I STILL DO! WITH A PASSION! BUT YOU CAN'T JUST IGNORE THE FACT HE SAVED MY LIFE. BESIDES, UNLIKE OTHER COMMIES, HE HAPPENS TO BE AN OKAY GUY.

YEAH, BUT IF HE'S SUCH A NICE GUY, WHY'D HE BECOME A TERRORIST? WELL, IT WASN'T REALLY HIS FAULT...

HIS FAMILY PRESSURED HIM INTO IT...

HI, DAD! YOUR SON'S HOME!

SON? WHAT SON?.. I HAVE NO SON.

ALL I HAVE IS A PARASITIC OFFSPRING WHO, YEAR AFTER YEAR, MANAGES TO PASS HIS COURSES JUST IN TIME FOR ME TO SHELL OUT YET ANOTHER FOUR THOUSAND DOLLARS.

:SIGH:

SON? ME? NO,.. NO, I HAVE NO SON.

MARK, I HAVE PREPARED A BILL FOR YOU.

EXCUSE ME, FATHER?

TWO YEARS OF COLLEGE @ $4500. PER YEAR; FOUR YEARS OF SECONDARY SCHOOL @ $3500; EIGHT YEARS OF PRIMARY SCHOOL @ $3380; NURSERY SCHOOL @ $2135..

THREE YEARS OF SUMMER CAMP @ $700; CLOTHING FOR NINETEEN YEARS $2710; FOOD, FOR SAME, $7,345.53; CHRISTMAS PRESENTS, $920.60; TOTAL, $65,251.13.

PAY UP.

WILL YOU TAKE A CHECK?

DAD, I'VE LOOKED OVER YOUR BILL. IT'S RIDICULOUS.

HOW COULD I POSSIBLY PAY YOU $65,251.13? I'VE EVEN ALREADY SPENT NEXT MONTH'S ALLOWANCE.

...THE WHOLE THING IS UNBELIEVABLY CHILDISH ANYWAY. I REFUSE TO PAY YOU AND YOU CAN'T MAKE ME!

YOU'LL HEAR FROM MY LAWYER IN THE MORNING.

MOTHER, YOU HAVE BEEN ABSOLUTELY **NO** HELP IN THIS RECENT MADNESS.

I'M SORRY, DEAR.

MOTHER, HOW CAN YOU STAND MEEKLY BY AND WITNESS THIS RIDICULOUS CHARADE?!

I'M SORRY, DEAR.

MOTHER, I DON'T UNDERSTAND YOU. HOW CAN YOU DEFEND A HUSBAND WHO IS TRYING TO EXTORT MONEY FROM HIS OWN SON?

I'M GETTING A 30% CUT, DEAR.

HEE, HEE.

HI, SARGE. WHAT'S UP? GOT SOME NEW ORDERS HERE FOR B.D.!

WHAT ORDERS, SARGE? AS PART OF THE NEW TROOP WITHDRAWALS, YOU'RE SCHEDULED TO LEAVE VIETNAM THE DAY AFTER TOMORROW.

HE SO WANTED TO BE PART OF THE RESIDUAL FORCE.

GEORGE, WOULD YOU PLEASE EXPLAIN THIS CRAZY WAR TO ME? I DON'T GET IT!—A BUNCH OF HARVARD GRADUATES THOUGHT UP THIS WHOLE WAR...

...BUT THEY SEND A BUNCH OF DRAFTED HIGH SCHOOL GRADUATES TO FIGHT IT! FINALLY, THEY GET A GUY, ME, WHO WANTS TO STAY, AND THEY WITHDRAW HIM! IT'S JUST NOT FAIR!

WELL, SURE IT'S UNFAIR! ALL WARS ARE UNFAIR! I KNOW, I KNOW!

...BUT THIS WAR HAD SUCH PROMISE!!

YOU'RE BEING WITHDRAWN?! GEE, THAT MUST BE VERY DISAPPOINTING FOR YOU.

WELL, IT WAS AT FIRST, BUT I FIGURE THERE'S A GOOD CHANCE I'LL GET TRANSFERRED TO GERMANY. YOU KNOW, THE COLD WAR!!

THE COLD WAR'S A WHOLE DIFFERENT SCENE, PHRED! WHO KNOWS, MAYBE I'LL GET TO FIGHT THE KRAUTS!

WE GOOKS ARE GOING TO MISS YOU, B.D.

SO LONG, KID, HOPE THEY SEND YOU TO GERMANY LIKE YOU WANT. ME, TOO. THANKS FOR BRINGING ME DOWN TO THE AIRPORT, GEORGE.

BLAM! BOOM!

RAID! LET'S GET OUT OF HERE! HEY, GEORGE, DON'T WORRY! IT'S JUST PHRED SAYING GOODBY! ZING!

A TWENTY-ONE MORTAR SALUTE.

WHOOSH!

I DIDN'T REALLY WANT YOU ANYWAY, YOU STUPID MOURNING CLOAK!

WELL, I JUST CAUGHT MESELF THE COVETED MOURNING CLOAK BUTTERFLY! GUESS WE CAN HEAD BACK!

O.K.

BUTTERFLIES! NOW WHAT'S THAT GOT TO DO WITH ANYTHING? I DON'T WANT TO GROW UP TO BE A LEPIDOPTERIST! I WANT TO BE A POWER BROKER!

A WHAT?

YOU KNOW, THE MAN IN CONTROL! BOY, WOULD I MAKE SOME CHANGES. I'D RULE OVER A PEACEFUL COUNTRY OF HARMONY AND BROTHERHOOD!.. I THINK I'D HAVE HUEY P. NEWTON AS MY PRIME MINISTER, MILES DAVIS AS MY ATTORNEY GENERAL, AND BILL COSBY AS HEAD OF H.E.W.!

I MIGHT KEEP OL' NIXON AND SOME OF THEM SENATORS WHERE THEY ARE, BUT JUST FOR LAUGHS, 'CAUSE IT'D BE A PUPPET GOVERNMENT!

HEE, HEE! HA, HA, HA!

YOU'RE A CRAZY DUDE, RUFUS.

I CAN DREAM, CAN'T I?

PAPER!

WHY, THANK YOU!!

AMAZING! HERE'S ANOTHER ARTICLE WITH EVIDENCE WHICH CONTRADICTS THE OFFICIAL EXPLANATION OF THE KENT STATE SHOOTINGS!

SO?

WHAT DO YOU MEAN, "SO"? DOESN'T ALL THAT DECEIT IRK YOU?!

SURE. BUT THE ATTORNEY GENERAL HAS CLOSED THE CASE!

EXACTLY! MITCHELL CLOSED THE CASE FOR POLITICAL REASONS, KNOWING HE COULD JIVE A WEARY PUBLIC! THINK ABOUT THAT!

I'D RATHER NOT. IT'S FOOLISH TO COMMIT YOURSELF TO WORRYING ABOUT JUST ONE ATROCITY...

FOR EXAMPLE, IF I WERE TO GET MYSELF INTO A STATE OF IMPOTENT RAGE OVER KENT STATE, WHICH WAS OVER A YEAR AGO, MY INDIGNATION OVER ATTICA WOULD BE COMPROMISED.

11-28

PERSONALLY, I THINK JOHN MITCHELL DID US A FAVOR BY DISMISSING KENT STATE, BECAUSE NOW WE CAN CONCENTRATE ON FRESHER, MORE RECENT, TRAGEDIES.

GBTrudeau

HAND ME THE COMICS, WILL YA?

HEADS UP! —

SAY, MIKE DID YOU GO OUT TO A PARTY ON NEW YEAR'S EVE?

NO. JUST COULDN'T GET UP FOR IT.

I THOUGHT ABOUT GOING, AND THEN I THOUGHT, NO, BY GOLLY, THAT SURELY WOULD BE A BIG WASTE OF TIME!

IT'S RIDICULOUS, BERNIE! NO ONE EVER REALLY ENJOYS THOSE THINGS! DRINKING AND PRETENDING TO HAVE FUN, THAT'S ALL IT IS!

IT'S FORCED FUN! EVERYONE THINKS HE SHOULD BE CELEBRATING AND CARRYING ON, WHICH, AS A CONCEPT, IS BASICALLY SELF-CONSCIOUS AND IMMATURE!

YESSIR, NEW YEAR'S EVE IS THE DUMBEST, STUPIDEST, BORINGEST, TIME OF THE ENTIRE YEAR!!

COULDN'T GET A DATE AGAIN, HUH?

I CAN'T UNDERSTAND IT..

ALAS! THE PICNIC'S OVER.

GENTLEMEN, AS YOUR PRESIDENT, IT IS WITH A HEAVY HEART THAT I SEND YOU OUT INTO THE WORLD TODAY.

YES, IT ALWAYS SEEMS TO ME THAT EVEN AFTER FOUR TOUGH YEARS OF ARTS, LETTERS AND SCIENCES, THE GRADUATING CLASS IS **STILL** NOT READY TO BEAR UP UNDER THE PRESSURES OF THIS SOCIETY.

TODAY YOU ARE HAPPY MEN — SAFE AND CONTENT IN THE KNOWLEDGE THAT IT IS SHEEPSKIN DAY, THE DAY WHEN ALL OF YOU CAN REJOICE IN A JOB WELL DONE!

WELL, GENTLEMEN, SUCH ATTITUDES ARE PERMISSIBLE TODAY! BUT WHAT ABOUT TOMORROW? THIS IS THE FUNDAMENTAL QUESTION — YOU MUST NOW ASK YOURSELVES!—**WHAT** DO YOU INTEND TO BE DOING THIS TIME **TOMORROW**?!

SMOKING A LOT OF GRASS.

HA, HA! YEA! YEA! CLAP! HA, HA! HA! HA, HA! CLAP! HA! HA!

THIS GETS HARDER EVERY YEAR.

WELL, WE'VE GOT TO GET BACK ON THE ROAD, ZONKER.

I SURE HATE TO GO BEFORE ALL THE DELEGATES ACTUALLY LEAVE. SOMETHING IMPORTANT MIGHT HAPPEN AND I'LL MISS IT.

MR. CHAIRMAN, THE DELEGATION FROM RHODE ISLAND REQUESTS PERMISSION TO SEND OUT FOR SOME PIZZA!

I'M OFF.

TAKE CARE.

ZONKER! A POSTCARD FROM MIAMI HAS ARRIVED FOR YOU!

FOR ME? O, HAPPY DAY!

"DEAR ZONKER, I MUST SAY, OL' BOY, YOU CUT A FINE FIGURE AT THE CONVENTION. YOUR PRESENCE WAS A REAL ADDITION.

"AS HARVEST TIME APPROACHES, I WISH YOU WELL WITH YOUR WHEAT PATCH. GOOD LUCK, KID, YOU'RE A RARE HUMAN BEING."

IT'S FROM ME!

SO THIS IS YOUR FIRST VISIT TO SAN FRANCISCO, EH, PILGRIM?

YUP... SAY, ARE THOSE GIRLS DANCING UP THERE REALLY CO-EDS?

YOUR SIGN OUTSIDE! IT SAID "BEAUTIFUL, EXCITING CO-EDS."

WHAT?

OH,...YEAH! SURE! THEY'RE CO-EDS! SUZIE, THE BLONDE THERE, IS A CUM LAUDE FROM WELLESLEY, AND DORIS IS A PHYSICS MAJOR AT STANFORD, AND TIGER-LIPS, THE ONE WITH THE LEGS, SHE'S MATRICULATING AT YALE THIS FALL.

WHY? YOU A COLLEGE MAN?

HEY, ARE YOU A SIGHT FOR SORE EYES!

HOW NOW?

DO YOU REALIZE I'VE BEEN HERE IN SAN FRANCISCO TWO DAYS, AND YOU'RE THE FIRST STREET PERSON I'VE SEEN?! IMAGINE!

HEY, MAN, YOU GOT ANY ACID ON YOU? DO YOU? SURE YOU DO!

LET ME HAVE A FEW PUFFS, O.K.?

CHECK!

Panel 1: MA'AM, WE'VE COME ALMOST 400 MILES SINCE YOU STOPPED US. BEFORE WE GO ANY FURTHER, MAYBE YOU BETTER TELL US WHO YOU ARE AND WHERE YOU WANT TO GO...

Panel 2: FAIR ENOUGH, BOYS. MY NAME IS JOANIE CAUCUS AND I'M RUNNING AWAY FROM MY HUSBAND CLINTON. IN BRIEF, I GOT FED UP WITH THE MEANINGLESS ROLES THAT DEFINED MY LIFE.

Panel 3: I WANT TO FIND A NEW TOWN WHERE I CAN START A NEW LIFE... A PLACE WHERE I CAN LIVE OUT A GRACEFUL REPRIEVAL, A PLACE WHERE I CAN BEGIN ANEW.

Panel 4: CLEVELAND, SAY. HMM..

Panel 5: MS. CAUCUS — IF YOU DON'T MIND A PERSONAL QUESTION, WHEN DID YOU FIRST START HAVING DIFFICULTIES WITH YOUR HUSBAND CLINTON?

Panel 6: WELL, MIKE, IT'S DIFFICULT TO PINPOINT IT, BUT I GUESS IT MIGHT HAVE BEEN ONE NIGHT LAST SUMMER, WHEN HIS BOWLING BUDDIES CAME TO DINNER...

Panel 7: AT THE END OF THE MEAL, ONE OF HIS FRIENDS COMPLIMENTED ME ON MY FRENCH FRIES. CLINTON LEANED BACK IN HIS CHAIR, AND SAID WITH A BIG, STUPID GRIN, "MY WIFE, I THINK I'LL KEEP HER!"

Panel 8: I BROKE HIS NOSE.

Panel 9: HOME! HOME!

Panel 10: HOME! HELLOOO! WALDEN

Panel 11: ZONKER! HEEE WACKITY DO, DO, DOO! -BOING!

Panel 12: HOME? HOME. LET ME LOOK AT YOU! O.K.

Panel 13: SO THAT'S OUR DEAL — IF YOU HELP WITH THE COMMUNE, YOU CAN STAY UNTIL YOU FIND SOME SORT OF JOB! MIKE, I CAN'T THANK YOU ENOUGH...

Panel 14: BUT IN ALL FAIRNESS, I MUST WARN YOU — WE HAVE SOME VERY WEIRD PEOPLE IN OUR GROUP. OH, THAT'S ALRIGHT, DEAR, I...

Panel 15: KABOOM!!!

Panel 16: LOOK, THINK IT OVER... SURPRISE!

GIRLS, I'D LIKE TO TALK TO YOU ABOUT GROWING UP TO BE MOMMIES.

GROWING UP TO BE A MOMMY IS ONE OF THE MOST WONDERFUL THINGS A LITTLE GIRL CAN WANT TO DO. BUT... THERE ARE OTHER THINGS IN LIFE SHE CAN DO AS WELL...

FOR INSTANCE, SHE CAN WORK HER HEAD OFF AND SHOW ALL THOSE ARROGANT BOYS THAT SHE'S JUST AS CAPABLE AND INTELLIGENT AND CREATIVE AS ANY LITTLE STUD AROUND!

YOU'RE A "LIBBIE," AREN'T YOU, MS. CAUCUS?

YOU BET, HONEY.

MS. CAUCUS, WE BOYS HAVE BEEN NOTICING A BIG CHANGE IN THE GIRLS LATELY. THEY'VE BEEN ACTING LIKE BOYS!

WELL, DEAR, I'M NOT SURE YOU BOYS ARE BEING QUITE FAIR...

A GREAT LADY, SIMONE DE BEAUVOIR, ONCE SAID THAT THERE ARE TWO KINDS OF PEOPLE; HUMAN BEINGS AND WOMEN. AND WHEN WOMEN START ACTING LIKE HUMAN BEINGS, THEY ARE ACCUSED OF TRYING TO BE MEN.

YEAH... BUT... BUT... UM....

SIMONE DE BEAUVOIR'S GOT YOUR NUMBER, SLIM.

HAVE YOU BEEN DOWN TO VISIT JOANIE AT THE DAY CARE CENTER YET?

NO... HOW'S HER NEW JOB COMING?

OKAY, I GUESS.... SHE'S BEEN ADMINISTERING CONSCIOUSNESS-RAISING SESSIONS TO THE GIRLS...

TERRIFIC!

I DUNNO.. JOANIE MAY BE ASKING TOO MUCH OF LITTLE GIRLS OF THAT AGE..

NONSENSE! I'M SURE SHE'S HANDLING IT BEAUTIFULLY.

WAAH! I DON'T WANNA BE A BUILDING CONTRACTOR!

NOW DEAR...

I'M SORRY, MIKE, I CAN'T WORK FOR McGOVERN. B.D. AND I ARE FOR NIXON.

TELL ME, BOOPSIE, DO YOU BELIEVE IN PEACE AND PROSPERITY AND FAIR PLAY?

WELL, YES, OF COURSE.

DO YOU BELIEVE IN THE PROMISE OF THE AMERICAN SPIRIT, AND THE DIGNITY OF ALL MEN AND WOMEN?

SURE I DO!

THEN YOU'RE FOR GEORGE McGOVERN. HE'S FOR ALL THOSE THINGS.

WOW... AND I THOUGHT I WAS FOR NIXON.

WELL, YOU GOTTA THINK THESE THINGS THROUGH...

HMM.. MAIL'S LATE TODAY.

MAILMAN!

ZONKER! HEY, WHAT GIVES, HOMBRE?

OL' RALPHIE'S SICK. I TOLD HIM I'D TAKE OVER FOR HIM THIS WEEK!

OH, HERE'S YOUR MAIL, KID! FRANKLY I'VE SEEN BETTER. YOUR MOM IS FINE, BUT YOUR DATE'S OFF FOR THIS WEEKEND, AND YOU FAILED ENGLISH! WELL, SEE YA!

"NEITHER RAIN NOR SNOW NOR SLEET!.."

IT'S ABOUT TIME YOU GOT HERE, MAILMAN! I'M EXPECTING A LETTER FROM MY DAUGHTER AT WELLESLEY!

SHE'S ONLY A FRESHMAN, BUT SHE'S DOING MIGHTY WELL! MY CATHY IS REALLY SOMETHING SPECIAL!

CATHY? SAY, SHE MUST BE THE ONE WHO WROTE YOU THAT SHE'S NOW LIVING WITH A SAXOPHONE PLAYER IN BOSTON!

WHAT?!

SURE, CATHY, THAT'S RIGHT!

I THINK THIS RAIN, SNOW AND SLEET BUSINESS IS FINALLY GETTING TO ME. I WANT OUT!

I DON'T KNOW HOW POSTMEN CAN DO THIS ALL YEAR ROUND. I'VE ONLY BEEN AT IT ONE WEEK AND I'M EXHAUSTED!

AT LEAST I HAVEN'T MET UP WITH ANY FEROCIOUS DOGS! WE ITINERANT PUBLIC SERVANTS ARE TERRIFIED OF POOCHIES!

KNOCK! KNOCK!

YEAH?

WHO IS IT, BOY?

DAD? IT'S ME, MARK!

SAY, DAD, I'VE GOT GREAT NEWS! I JUST GOT MY GRADES AND GUESS WHAT? I MADE THE DEAN'S LIST! ISN'T THAT TERRIFIC?

DAD?.. DAD?..

DEAR?.. DEAR?..

'BYE, MOM! BE GOOD NOW!

SHE'S A COURAGEOUS SOUL, PHRED.

SHE CERTAINLY IS. SHE'S PUT IN THOUSANDS OF MILES ON THE ROAD OVER THE YEARS.

AND FOR A REFUGEE, SHE'S PRETTY RESOURCEFUL. SEE THAT KNAPSACK SHE'S GOT ON? SHE GOT THAT FROM AN ABANDONED FIREBASE.

WHERE'D SHE GET THE MOTORCYCLE?

I'M NOT SURE.

HEY! I THOUGHT THIS HAMLET LOOKED FAMILIAR! I USED TO GO TO SCHOOL HERE!

REALLY?

SURE! THIS WAS MY OLD SCHOOLHOUSE RIGHT IN FRONT OF US! OVER THERE WAS THE PLAY AREA!

WHAT MEMORIES THIS RUBBLE BRINGS BACK! ARITHMETIC, GEOGRAPHY, CHALK FIGHTS!... THIS WAS MY CLASSROOM RIGHT HERE!

HEY! MY OLD DESK!

MAN, THAT WAS SOME KINDA SHELLING! MUST HAVE BEEN SOME OF YOUR BOYS...

HEY, LOOK, PHRED! THERE'S A GUY OVER THERE WHO LOOKS HURT! MAYBE WE SHOULD GET HELP FOR HIM.

OH, NO NEED TO WORRY ABOUT HIM! HE'S JUST ONE OF MILLIONS OF CIVILIANS WHO HAVE BEEN WOUNDED OR KILLED IN THE LAST TEN YEARS!

WHAT'S EATING YOU?

...I'M SORRY... I'VE JUST GOT A BAD HEADACHE...

BLAM!

BOOM

YOU HEARTLESS AIR PIRATES!

I HOPE YOU CAN LIVE WITH IT! I HOPE YOU CAN LIVE WITH ALL THE DESTRUCTION AND CARNAGE YOU'VE BROUGHT TO MY LITTLE COUNTRY!!

DIDJA HEAR THE KNICKS TOOK TWO?

HEEY! THAT'S GREAT!

US 473

III/A Lasting Piece of the Action

Disengagements become rife, with mixed blessings for the disengaged. Phred, on his own now, finds himself traded to the Pathet Lao, but seeing the ghost of America haunting almost all of Indochina, he is inspired to return the memories by organizing an airlift of homeless Cambodians to Washington, allowing liberal congressmen, and even Georgetown matrons, to adopt their very own refugees. But before patronization comes recrimination—whether at the White House, toiling in the coils of Watergate, on the lecture circuit with a flamboyantly penitent Jeb Magruder, or the more traditional mumblings at the class of '43 reunions. All such turns and pangs are witnessed bucolically by the denizens of Walden Commune, though not without contributions of their own—such as Mark taking to the airwaves as a DJ with Watergate profiles ("Guilty, guilty, guilty!"), and Joanie working wonders at the day-care center in extracting sexism from her scruffy charges.

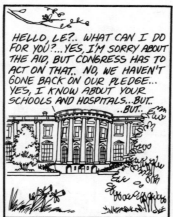

HEY, WHERE'S OL' MARCUS TODAY? I THOUGHT HE WAS COMING OUT FOR AN AFTERNOON DIP!

NOPE. HE HAD TO GO BARTEND TODAY AT THE REUNIONS.

BARTEND?

YEAH. HE WANTED TO WORK FOR ONE OF THE MORE RECENT CLASSES, BUT HE GOT STUCK WITH THE CLASS OF '43.

OH, NO!

AND DON'T GET ANY HAIR IN MY COCKTAIL, KID!

YESSIR.

...AFTER THAT, I JOINED MERRILL FUNDS, AND IT'S BEEN GRAVY EVER SINCE! ...BUT, HOWIE.. HOW ABOUT YOU? WHAT HAVE YOU BEEN UP TO ALL THESE YEARS?

ME?.. OH, I STILL HAVEN'T MADE UP MY MIND WHAT I WANT TO DO YET.

HEE HEE! HEE!

AND WHAT'S SO FUNNY ABOUT THAT, MAY I ASK?!

HOWIE, THIS IS OUR THIRTIETH REUNION.

I JUST DON'T WANT TO RUSH INTO ANYTHING!..

HOWIE, PERHAPS IT'S NONE OF MY BUSINESS, BUT DON'T YOU THINK IT'S ABOUT TIME YOU STARTED LOOKING FOR A JOB?

I MEAN, A MAN'S GOT TO HAVE SOME LIFE'S WORK. UNLIKE MOST OF YOUR CLASSMATES, HOWIE, YOU'VE JUST WASTED YOUR LIFE AWAY!

NONSENSE!

IN THE LAST THIRTY YEARS, I HAVE WATCHED THOUSANDS OF SUNSETS; I'VE PAINTED STILL-LIFES OF FERNS AND INDIAN CORN; I'VE READ THE VERSES OF MILTON, AND I'VE TAKEN LONG WALKS IN THE BERKSHIRES! WHAT HAVE YOU DONE THAT WAS SO GREAT?

WHY, HOWARD, YOU OL' HIPPY, YOU.

DAMN STRAIGHT!

SAY, FRANKIE, WHAT LINE DID YOU FINALLY END UP IN?

WELL, I'VE BEEN WORKING MOSTLY IN DRUGS.

OH? YOU'RE IN PHARMACEUTICS?

NOPE. I DEAL. IT'S NOT SO GREAT FROM A MORAL POINT OF VIEW, BUT TERRIFIC FINANCIALLY.

I REMEMBER HOW YOU GUYS AT BETA ALWAYS SAID I'D BE A SHARP OPERATOR. I THOUGHT ABOUT THAT THE NIGHT I MADE MY FIRST SCORE. WHAT IRONY!

BUT ENOUGH ABOUT ME! HOW'S GINNY AND THE KIDS?!

GOOD NEWS, KIDDIES! TIME FOR ANOTHER EXCLUSIVE WBBY "WATERGATE PROFILE"! TODAY'S OBITUARY— JOHN MITCHELL!

JOHN MITCHELL, THE FORMER U.S. ATTORNEY GENERAL, HAS IN RECENT WEEKS BEEN REPEATEDLY LINKED WITH BOTH THE WATERGATE CAPER AND ITS COVER-UP.

IT WOULD BE A DISSERVICE TO MR. MITCHELL AND HIS CHARACTER TO PREJUDGE THE MAN, BUT EVERYTHING KNOWN TO DATE COULD LEAD ONE TO CONCLUDE HE'S GUILTY!

THAT'S GUILTY! GUILTY, GUILTY, GUILTY!!

HOLY MOLY, CAMPERS! TIME FOR ANOTHER WBBY "WATERGATE PROFILE"! TODAY'S COVER-UP CUTIE IS... JOHN EHRLICHMAN!

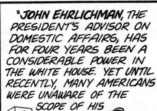

"JOHN EHRLICHMAN, THE PRESIDENT'S ADVISOR ON DOMESTIC AFFAIRS, HAS FOR FOUR YEARS BEEN A CONSIDERABLE POWER IN THE WHITE HOUSE. YET UNTIL RECENTLY, MANY AMERICANS WERE UNAWARE OF THE SCOPE OF HIS DUTIES!

"ON THE AVERAGE DAY JOHN EHRLICHMAN USED TO CONSULT WITH MR. NIXON AT LEAST ONCE OR TWICE. IF THE WORD CAME DOWN HE WAS NEEDED, HE'D MAKE HIS WAY UP TO THE OVAL OFFICE WHERE HE WOULD INVARIABLY ENCOUNTER FELLOW STAFFER H.R. HALDEMAN!"

HALT! STOP OR I'LL SHOOT!

BOB! IT'S ME! IT'S ME!

HEEWACK! UN AUTRE "PROFILE" REQUEST! I'VE GOTTA HAND IT TO YOU, BOYS AND GIRLS — THERE'S BEEN TERRIFIC WATERGATE RESPONSE!

KEEP 'EM COMING, CAMPERS! GET THE FULL STORY — TRUTHS, INNUENDO, HEARSAY, THE WHOLE BIT— ON EVERYONE LINKED WITH THE NATION'S DARKEST SCANDAL!

FROM THE CUBAN BURGLARS TO THE CHIEF EXECUTIVE HIMSELF, IF YOU'VE GOT A FAVORITE WATERGATE CONSPIRATOR— AND YOU WANT TO KNOW MORE ABOUT HIM— REMEMBER TO PHONE IN YOUR REQUEST TO WBBY! THAT'S WBBY!!

OKAY! PROFILE OF JOHN DEAN III GOING OUT TO JOEY WITH HUGS FROM DONNA!

WELL, MOTHER O' MINE, IT'S TIME I LEFT FOR LAOS. I JUST GOT MY MARCHING ORDERS FROM THE PATHET LAO.

NOW YOU BE SURE TO WRITE ME IN... HEY! WHAT'S THIS?

IT'S A GOING-AWAY PRESENT! MOM, WHAT A THOUGHTFUL THING TO DO! HONESTLY...

"THE ALL-NEW TOMMY TOURIST GUIDE TO LAOS— 1961."

IT WAS ON SALE!

"UPON YOUR EXIT FROM THE **HO CHI MINH** TRAIL, TURN LEFT ONTO THE SCENIC MOUNTAIN PATH WHICH TRAVERSES THE HIGH COUNTRYSIDE."

"IF THE FERRY OVER THE MEANDERING **MEKONG** ISN'T WORKING, YOU MAY HAVE TO GET YOUR FEET WET. BE SURE TO BRING ALONG SOME DRY, LIGHTWEIGHT SUMMER CLOTHES FOR WHEN YOU REACH THE OTHER SIDE."

"A QUICK SCRAMBLE UP THE BEAUTIFUL **DINO-LINO** CLIFF FORMATION AND YOU SHOULD BE ABLE TO SPOT A SMALL LEDGE 80 YARDS ABOVE YOU. A SHORT, SPIRITED HIKE, AND THE TOURIST WILL SOON FIND HIMSELF AT THE TOP."

"WELCOME TO LAOS."

SIR?.. OH, SIR?..

PARDON US, SIR! WE ARE DESTITUTE, HUNGRY REFUGEES ON OUR WAY TO VIENTIANE! TAKE **PITY** ON US!

WE HAVE NOT EATEN IN **DAYS**! COULD NOT SOME OF US SHARE IN THE HOT RICE DINNER YOU HAVE PREPARED FOR YOURSELF?

UM...SURE. HOW MANY ARE THERE OF YOU?

135,000.

"ON YOUR LEFT, YOU SHOULD NOW SEE THE FAMOUS "**JUMPING JARS INN**." THIS QUAINT LITTLE RESTAURANT WITH ITS SIDEWALK TABLES HAS BEEN A FAVORITE WITH VISITORS FOR YEARS."

"BE SURE TO ASK FOR THE PROPRIETOR, 'LOO'! HE'LL BE DELIGHTED TO SERVE YOU ONE OF HIS TASTY, TANGY PUNCHES FOR WHICH HE IS RENOWNED THROUGHOUT THE PROVINCE."

"LOO"?

SORRY, MAN, WE'RE CLOSED.

AW, C'MON, LOO! CAN'T YOU EVEN FIX ME A LIGHT SNACK?

LOOK! I TOLD YOU! I'M **CLOSED**! I'VE BEEN BOMBED OUT OF BUSINESS!

LISTEN TO THIS, LOO: "WHILE THE LAOTIANS ARE A PROUD AND FIERCELY TENACIOUS PEOPLE, THEIR MOST OUT-STANDING CHARACTERISTIC IS **GENEROSITY**!

"WHETHER FOR A FRIEND IN NEED OR A PASSING STRANGER, THE LAOTIANS ARE ALWAYS QUICK ON THE DRAW WHEN IT COMES TO **KINDNESS, COMPASSION,** AND LENDING A **HELPING HAND**!

"FURTHERMORE..."

ALRIGHT ALREADY! I'LL TURN ON THE GRILL!

WELL, HENRY?..

MR. PRESIDENT, I REALIZE THE SITUATION **IS** DETERIORATING OVER THERE, BUT I'M AFRAID ABSOLUTELY **NO ONE** ACCEPTS "PROTECTIVE REACTION" AS A CREDIBLE CONCEPT THESE DAYS.

HMM... WELL, WHAT ABOUT MY OTHER IDEA?

SIR?

"CAMBODIAZATION."

FORGET IT.

WILL THERE BE ANYTHING ELSE THIS MORNING, MR. PRESIDENT?

NO, NO,.. I GUESS NOT, HAIG..

YOU SEEM A LITTLE DEPRESSED THIS MORNING, SIR..

≥ SIGH ≤.. I AM, OLD FRIEND, I AM...

HAIG.. YOU KNOW WHAT I NEED RIGHT NOW? I NEED SOMETHING TO BOOST MY MORALE, TO PICK UP MY SPIRITS...

HOW ABOUT IF I SEND OUT FOR SOME P.O.W.'S, SIR?

WHY... YES! THAT WOULD BE NICE!

WE INTERRUPT THE SENATE WATERGATE HEARINGS TO BRING YOU THIS SPECIAL BULLETIN.

TODAY ON THE PRE-EMPTED SOAP OPERA, "AS THE HOSPITAL TURNS," DR. HARDIN FINALLY DECIDED TO DIVORCE HIS WIFE RACHEL, AFTER FIVE YEARS OF MARRIAGE! A BITTER CUSTODY FIGHT IS EXPECTED.

TO REPEAT: DR. HARDIN IS GETTING A DIVORCE FROM RACHEL! THAT'S A FINAL.

WE NOW RETURN TO OUR REGULARLY SCHEDULED BROADCAST.

LEONARD, AS MY COUNSEL, I THINK IT'S ABOUT TIME YOU TOOK A LOOK AT THESE TRANSCRIPTS OF THE SECRET TAPES...

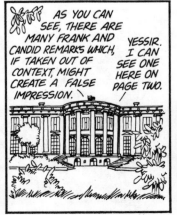
AS YOU CAN SEE, THERE ARE MANY FRANK AND CANDID REMARKS WHICH, IF TAKEN OUT OF CONTEXT, MIGHT CREATE A FALSE IMPRESSION.

YESSIR. I CAN SEE ONE HERE ON PAGE TWO.

WHICH ONE'S THAT?

"WELL, JOHN, HOW'S THE COVER-UP GOING?"

RIGHT! A GOOD EXAMPLE!

YESSIR. IT **COULD** BE MISINTERPRETED.

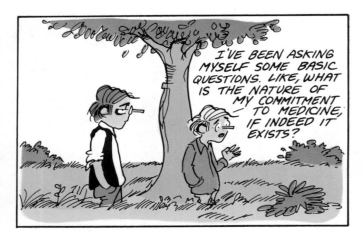

SAY, THOR, WHERE DO YOU WANT TO LIVE WHEN YOU GROW UP?

THE GOLD COAST.

YOU KNOW, THOR, I'VE BEEN NOTICING THAT YOU SPEAK MORE CLEARLY THAN MOST OF YOUR FRIENDS...

BY WHOSE STANDARDS, MIKE? YOURS?

WELL...

MIKE, THERE'S A GOOD BOOK I THINK YOU SHOULD READ. IT'S ABOUT AFRO-AMERICAN SPEECH...

SEE, PEOPLE HAVE ALWAYS BEEN CRITICAL OF BLACK LANGUAGE IRREGULARITIES. THEY CLAIM THAT WE BLACKS HAVE LAZY ARTICULATION.

THIS BOOK REFUTES THAT ACCUSATION EFFECTIVELY. THE AUTHOR HAS DOCUMENTED A CASE WHICH PROVES AFRO-AMERICAN SPEECH RHYTHMS ORIGINATE FROM THE INDIGENOUS LANGUAGES OF WESTERN AFRICA!

WOW.

REALLY?

SHO 'NUFF.

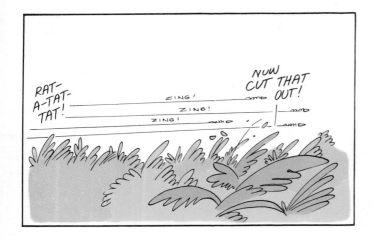

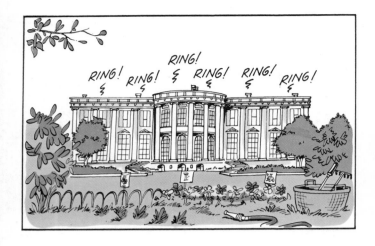

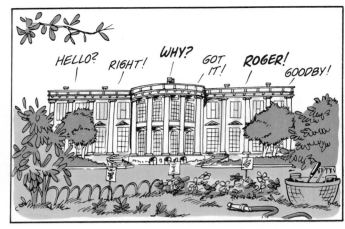

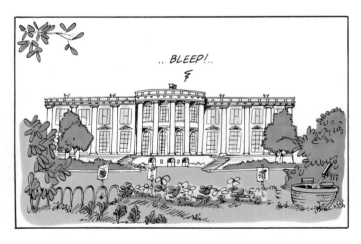

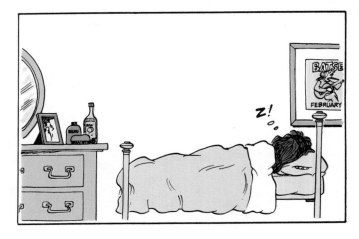

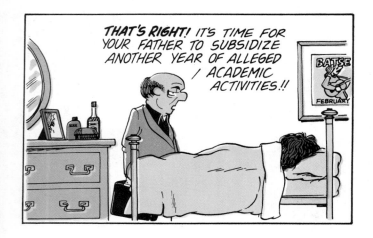

SAY, HOW MUCH LONGER 'TIL VACATION?

SEVEN DAYS, THREE HOURS, AND TWENTY MINUTES.

YOU KNOW, SOMETIMES I KIND OF MISS OL' TED AGNEW. I WONDER WHAT HE'S UP TO THESE DAYS...

SEARCH ME, LADY.

HE'S PROBABLY SPENDING HIS DECEMBER DAYS AT THE PALM SPRINGS HIDEAWAY OF AN AGING BUT CURIOUSLY UNRETIRED CROONER...

HE'S LICKING HIS WOUNDS, AND NO DOUBT STILL FEELS QUITE VICTIMIZED BY... "THE NEW POST-WATERGATE MORALITY"!

"THE NEW POST-WATERGATE MORALITY"... I WONDER WHAT HE MEANT BY THAT... WHAT EXACTLY **IS** "THE **NEW POST**-WATERGATE MORALITY"?

I MEAN, I FEEL THE SAME WAY ABOUT BRIBERY AND EXTORTION NOW AS I DID A YEAR AGO!

YEAH, WELL, YOU'RE WEIRD.

NONSENSE! TA, TA, FELLOW CITIZENS!

GOOD EVENING. WELCOME TO **ABC NEWS!**

HARRY'S ON VACATION, AND HOWARD'S ON ASSIGNMENT. FRANK IS ON THE ROAD.

SAM IS OFF THE AIR, TOM IS IN TRANSIT, AND TINA IS OUT TO LUNCH. I'M THE ONLY ONE LEFT HERE. MY NAME IS CARLOS; I WORK UPSTAIRS IN THE STOCK-ROOM.

HERE ARE TONIGHT'S HEADLINES..

BUT CONGRESSMAN, YOU HAVE TO VIEW THE SECRET CAMBODIAN BOMBINGS IN PERSPECTIVE, IN THE PROPER TIME-FRAME!

TIME-FRAME, GENERAL?

YES, SIR.. YOU SEE, THERE WERE DOZENS OF BOMBINGS ON CAMPUSES ALL ACROSS THE COUNTRY..

NATURALLY, THAT KIND OF ATMOSPHERE LED A FEW WELL-INTENTIONED BUT OVERZEALOUS OFFICIALS TO BELIEVE THAT BOMBING WAS AN ACCEPTABLE MEANS OF SOCIAL CHANGE.

OH, **THAT** TIME-FRAME!

YES, SIR.

WHAT IS IT, HAIG?

SIR, IT'S ABOUT THE HOUSE HEARINGS ON THE SECRET CAMBODIAN BOMBINGS...

WE NEED TO KNOW MORE ABOUT THE RAIDS, SIR. THEY SAY NOBODY BUT YOU KNEW ABOUT THEM.

IT'S NOT TRUE! I TOLD EVERYBODY WHO HAD A NEED OR RIGHT TO KNOW!

YES, SIR, BUT WHO? YOU'VE GOT TO BE MORE SPECIFIC.

WELL, LET ME SEE... THE PILOTS, OF COURSE ...

YES, GO ON...

JOANIE, I WONDER IF YOU'D BREAK YOUR DATING MORATORIUM AND GO OUT WITH ME TONIGHT..

THANKS, SCOT, BUT I'D REALLY RATHER NOT...

GEE, I THINK YOU'LL REGRET IT, JOANIE. I REALLY DO..

WHAT DO YOU MEAN, SCOT?

WELL, YOU SEE, I JUST HAPPEN TO HAVE TWO TICKETS TO THE JEB MAGRUDER CONCERT..

SCOT! HONEY!

HEE, HEE... AT WHAT POINT IN TIME SHALL I PICK YOU UP?

MOSELY! GET YOUR TAIL OVER HERE!

MOSELY, DID YOU PLANT THIS MICROPHONE IN THE DEFENDANT'S HOTEL ROOM? BECAUSE IF YOU DID, I'M GOING TO HAVE TO THROW THIS WHOLE CASE OUT OF COURT!

WHAT?! A MIKE IN THE DEFENDANT'S ROOM?! WHY I'M SHOCKED TO LEARN OF THIS THING! TRULY!

OKAY, KID, BEAT IT.

THANKS, YOUR HONOR!

JUDGE, I KNOW HOW YOU FEEL ABOUT ILLEGAL TAPS, AND.. I'M.. I'M REALLY SORRY IT HAPPENED..

I GUESS I JUST GOT OVER-ZEALOUS IN MY PURSUIT OF A CONVICTION..

I KNOW— I'M A NEW D.A., AND I SHOULDN'T HAVE BLOWN MY FIRST BIG CASE, BUT..

YOU HAD IT IN THE BAG, MAN, YOU HAD IT IN THE BAG!

YESSIR..

HELLO?.. YES, THIS IS THE PRESIDENT.. WHO?.. MR. BREZHNEV!?... YOU'RE WHERE?.. AT THE AIRPORT?..

GEE, MR. CHAIRMAN, WE DIDN'T EXPECT YOU UNTIL NEXT WEEK! I'M SORRY WE DIDN'T HAVE ANY BANDS OR ANYTHING OUT THERE...

MY APPOINTMENTS SECRETARY MUST HAVE SLIPPED UP OR SOMETHING.. THINGS GET SO HECTIC AROUND HERE SOMETIMES.. IT MUST BE LIKE THAT AT THE KREMLIN, TOO, HUH?.. YEAH.. YEAH..RIGHT.

WELL, LOOK, LEONID— WHY DON'T YOU GRAB A CAB AND COME ON IN?

MR. NIXON, WITHOUT MEANING TO PRY, I AM MOST CURIOUS AS TO HOW YOU'VE MANAGED TO DEAL WITH THE PRESS DURING THIS NASTY PERIOD...

LEONID, I'D BE HAPPY TO SHOW YOU... ZIEGLER!

RON, ANSWER THIS QUESTION: "RON, WILL THE PRESIDENT TESTIFY BEFORE THE SENATE COMMITTEE?"

YESSIR, MR. NIXON?

TO BE RESPONSIVE AT THIS TIME, THOUGH I WILL SIMPLY SAY THAT, AS I SAID—AND THEREFORE THIS IS A REPEAT OF WHAT I SAID PREVIOUSLY—THAT WHICH I AM UNABLE TO OFFER IN RESPONSE IS BASED ON INFORMATION AVAILABLE TO MAKE NO SUCH STATEMENT!

VERY IMPRESSIVE!

WELL, WE LIKE HIM..

THE *MUSEUM!* WHAT HAPPENED TO IT? IT'S.. IT'S TOTALLY *DEMOLISHED!*

I KNOW, BOY, I KNOW! I WAS THE CURATOR.

YOU WRETCHED SOUL! DID THIS HAPPEN DURING THE SECRET BOMBINGS?

SECRET BOMBINGS? BOY, THERE WASN'T ANY *SECRET* ABOUT THEM! *EVERYONE* HERE KNEW! *I* DID, AND MY *WIFE,* SHE KNEW, TOO! SHE WAS WITH ME, AND I REMARKED ON THEM!

I SAID "LOOK, MARTHA, HERE COME THE BOMBS."

IT'S TRUE, HE DID.

YOU KNOW, BOSS, I JUST THOUGHT OF SOMETHING YOU COULD SEE — MY ALMA MATER, THE LOCAL UNIVERSITY!

YOU WENT TO COLLEGE?

FOR A WHILE. I DROPPED OUT, THOUGH.. HOW I GOT REALLY TURNED OFF TO IT.

HOW COME?

I DUNNO — JUST A WEIRD PLACE. LIKE ONCE WE HAD THIS ANTI-WAR SIT-IN, SO THEY SENT IN A COMPANY OF TROOPS WHO CLOSED THE SCHOOL DOWN AND EXECUTED THE ENTIRE FRESHMAN CLASS!

LOST A LOT OF GOOD FRAT PLEDGES THAT YEAR..

I'LL BET.

THERE YOU HAVE IT, BOSS. 300,000 WAR VICTIMS!

WOW! I CAN'T BELIEVE IT!

I'M AMAZED! AND I'M NO STRANGER TO REFUGEE CAMPS!

WELL, THIS IS THE BIGGEST IN ALL OF CAMBODIA.

EVEN THE CAMBODIANS ARE INCREDULOUS — FOLKS COME OUT HERE ALL THE TIME JUST TO SEE THE CAMP! IT'S CONSIDERED AN IMPORTANT SITE!

I JUST HOPE IT DOESN'T GET ALL TOURISTY.

MAN, JUST SEEING THE CONDITIONS HERE IS REALLY GETTING TO ME.. IT'S JUST NOT *FAIR!* SOMEONE SHOULD TAKE THE RESPONSIBILITY FOR VICTIMIZING ALL THESE PEOPLE!

YOU KNOW, IF WE COULD GET SOME OF THESE REFUGEES OVER TO WASHINGTON, WHERE THEY COULD.. ..WELL..*LOBBY* ON THEIR OWN BEHALF, I BET WE'D GET SOME ACTION THEN!

YEAH!

YOU GOT ANY IDEA HOW WE COULD GET 'EM OVER?

COME TO THINK OF IT, BOSS, I KNOW A LOCAL AUSSIE PILOT WHO OWES ME A FAVOR!

THEN IT'S *DECIDED!*

OKAY, LISTEN UP, PEOPLE!

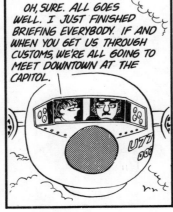

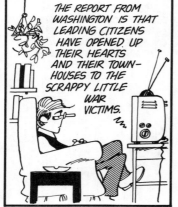

I AM AN OLD WOMAN, SIRS. I KNOW NOTHING OF POLITICS. I KNOW ONLY THAT THE AIRPLANE CAME AND DESTROYED MY VILLAGE.

BUT CAN YOU BE SURE IT WAS AN AMERICAN PLANE, MS. LOO? THIS, OF COURSE, IS OF VITAL IMPORTANCE!

YOU SEE, MS. LOO, THERE ARE MANY DIFFERENT KINDS OF PLANES — THERE ARE BIG ONES, LITTLE ONES, JET PLANES AND..

IT WAS A NAVY McDONNELL F4B-1 PHANTOM II. OH, YES, THAT'S OURS.

MR. PHRED, THE COMMITTEE WOULD LIKE TO THANK YOU FOR ORGANIZING SO EFFECTIVELY ALL THE TESTIMONY WE HAVE HEARD TO DATE.

NOW THEN, HAVE YOU ITEMIZED THOSE MEASURES YOU DEEM NECESSARY FOR A SHORT-TERM CESSATION OF THE SUFFERING OF SOUTHEAST ASIAN REFUGEES?

YES, SENATOR. COUNSEL AND I HAVE PREPARED A LIST OF WHAT WE FEEL ARE THE MINIMAL MATERIALS REQUIRED TO ALLEVIATE THE CURRENT CRISIS.. PROCEED.

3.5 MILLION SLEEPING BAGS... HOLD IT.

THE COMMITTEE WOULD LIKE TO THANK THE REFUGEE WITNESSES FOR THEIR MANY IN-SIGHTS INTO THE REFUGEE PROBLEM IN SOUTHEAST ASIA.

WE APPRECIATE THE TROUBLE YOU TOOK TO COME ALL THE WAY TO WASHINGTON, D.C., TO PROVIDE YOUR TESTIMONY.

ALL IN ALL, YOU'VE BEEN GREAT SPORTS, EVERY ONE OF YOU! I MEAN IT!

WHAT DO WE HAVE FOR THE WITNESSES, JOHNNIE? WELL, SENATOR, FOR THE LADIES, FROM SPEIDEL, THE LATEST IN WATCHBANDS!

ELLIE?.. WHAT'S WRONG, DEAR? IT'S MOTHER... SHE'S PREGNANT—AND DUE ANY DAY!

BUT.. THAT'S WONDER-FUL!.. NO, IT'S NOT. FIVE YEARS AGO IT WAS WONDERFUL. NOW IT'S JUST REDUNDANT.

YOU MEAN.. FOUR BROTHERS. FOUR OF THE MEANEST, MOST MISERABLE CREATURES EVER CONCEIVED!

OH DEAR... I'VE GOT TO GET HER TO CALL IT OFF!

GOODNESS KNOWS I TRIED TO TELL HER, JEAN! "MOMMY" I SAID, "WHAT'S WITH ALL THE BABIES? YOU WANT TO BE A HOUSE-WIFE ALL YOUR LIFE?"

BUT SHE KEEPS TURNIN' 'EM OUT! EVERY YEAR, JUST LIKE CLOCKWORK! IT'S REALLY *AMAZING!*

I DUNNO.. MAYBE I'LL JUST HAVE TO WORK ON MY FATHER INSTEAD..

AS I UNDERSTAND IT, HE FIGURES HEAVILY IN ALL THIS..

OH, YEAH?

MOMMY GOES INTO THE HOSPITAL TODAY. I GUESS I BETTER START THINKING POSITIVELY ABOUT MY NEWEST SIBLING..

GOOD IDEA, DEAR!

I JUST HOPE IT'S A SISTER. I *NEED* A SISTER!

ALSO, IT'S MORE "IN" TO BE A FEMALE THAN A MALE THESE DAYS! MUCH MORE FASHIONABLE.

IT IS?

SURE!

I DON'T THINK THERE'S ANY QUESTION ABOUT IT...

IT'S TRUE. I READ IT IN "TIME" LAST WEEK.

ELLIE! PHONE FOR YOU, DEAR!

HELLO?.. HI, DADDY!.. SHE *DID?* WHAT IS IT?!

IT'S A WOMAN!

"WOMAN"?

IT'S A BABY WOMAN!

SAY, THOR, DO YOU KNOW ANYTHING ABOUT THIS CHRISTMAS ROCK-PAGEANT SCOT'S PLANNING?

OH, SURE. IT'S REALLY SHAPIN' UP...

HE'S GOT ABOUT THIRTY NEIGHBORHOOD PEOPLE PAR-TICIPATING — MUSICIANS, ACTORS, LIGHT PEOPLE — YOU NAME IT!.. I MYSELF PLAY JOSEPH IN THE NATIVITY SCENE..

JOSEPH? YOU?!

YEAH, WELL, AT FIRST I REFUSED TO DO IT... BUT THEN I CHECKED OUT MARY AT THE REHEARSAL TODAY.

CUTE?

I'M TELLIN' YA — THE FOXIEST IN TOWN!

IV/Tripping Down the Hangout Route

Our passion for instant nostalgia would seem inexhaustible and cunning, especially in times of crisis. Taking two widely disparate cases in point, we have the Watergate Many reuning over Mrs. Dean's onion dip and serenading themselves as "Richard Nixon's Secret Tapes Club Band," while that other crisis, the one affecting everybody's gas tank, finds Mark Slackmeyer dusting off his revolutionary regalia preparatory to coaching some discontent truckers in the art of confrontation. And at the eyes of the two storms, things are positively medieval—as Fort Nixon digs in for the good of future Presidents, and the Energy Czar calls for hot wax and signet ring to allocate an extra five gallons for a mother's son forced to live two months at a turnpike Hot Shoppe. But *Time* marches on—indeed, it sends a totally credulous reporter to interview Zonker on "The New Hedonism"—and a few souls work to nobler purposes, though Joanie finds the road to law school more than a little rocky. But there are many ways to stonewall.

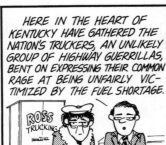

COULD YOU REPEAT THAT, YOUR CZARSHIP?

YOU HEARD ME — THE ENERGY CRISIS HAS ENDED!

IT'S ALL OVER, DON'T YOU SEE?! IT'S JUST NO GOOD PRETENDING! GO HOME TO YOUR FAMILIES — THERE'S NO STORY FOR YOU HERE ANYMORE!

FAR OUT.

ABOUT TIME.

NOW WAIT A MINUTE!

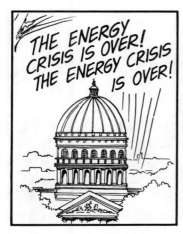

THE ENERGY CRISIS IS OVER! THE ENERGY CRISIS IS OVER!

DING! DONG!

GONG!

GONG!

LONG LIVE THE CZAR!! LONG LIVE THE CZAR!!

I DON'T KNOW WHY I DIDN'T THINK OF THIS EARLIER..

YEA!

GOOD MORNING. "TIME" MAGAZINE.

HELLO, THIS IS ROLAND BURTON HEDLEY, JR. I'M RETURNING MR. GRUNWALD'S CALL..

HI, ROLAND — WELCOME BACK TO THE STATES! TELL YOU WHY I CALLED — WE WANT YOU TO DIG UP SOME BACKGROUND FOR OUR ANNUAL "STATE-OF-THE-STUDENT" ESSAY.

HMM....SOUNDS INTRIGUING... I WONDER WHAT THE BEST APPROACH WOULD BE ... I KNOW! — I'LL GO INTERVIEW SOME UNDERGRADUATES!

GOOD PLAN, ROLAND.

I GOT SOME LEADS IN BOSTON...

HE WANTS TO INTERVIEW US FOR "TIME"?

YEAH, PROFESSOR GREEN TOLD HIM ABOUT WALDEN, SO HE WANTS TO COME OUT AND TALK WITH US ALL.

WHAT AN OPPORTUNITY!

THAT'S WHAT I WAS THINKIN'... LOOK SHARP, HERE HE COMES— ROLAND BURTON HEDLEY, JR.

HI, THERE, CHILDREN OF THE SEVENTIES!

INPUT! I'M LOOKING FOR INPUT!

YOU FIRST..

To: Photo Editor
From: Roland Burton Hedley, Jr.

This is Zonker Harris, 19, member of Walden.

Walden Commune—located about ½ mile from campus..

This is the backyard marijuana plant, which Zonker claims yields the highest grade grass in New England!

ROLAND, THAT'S A **LILAC** BUSH!

IT IS?..

ROLAND, I CAN'T BELIEVE THAT MOST COLLEGE STUDENTS HAVE BECOME SO **DECADENT!** ARE YOU **SURE** YOU VERIFIED THIS TREND ACROSS THE COUNTRY?

NO. I DIDN'T HAVE TO.

YOU DIDN'T **HAVE TO?!** WHAT DO YOU MEAN?!

THE STUDENTS I TALKED TO GAVE ME THEIR **WORD** OF **HONOR** THAT THEY REPRESENTED A NATIONAL TREND.

ROLAND, WHAT DID YOU COVER AT THE SAIGON BUREAU?

SPORTS.

CLACKITY!
CLAK! **CLACKITY! CLACK**

TIME
The New Hedonism

EXTRA! LATEST STUDENT MOOD!

"SEX! SEX AND PEYOTE!" HE REPLIED.

I'M IN **BIG** TROUBLE..

MAN, I NEVER **DREAMED** HE'D PRINT ALL THAT STUFF! IT'S ABSOLUTELY **INCREDIBLE!**

ROLAND BURTON HEDLEY, JR. REALLY TAKES THE **PRIZE**, YOU KNOW THAT?! WE COULD HAVE TOLD HIM WE WERE **EXPATRIATED ZULUS** AND HE WOULD HAVE BELIEVED US!

AW, C'MON, DON'T WORRY ABOUT IT, ZONK — YOU'RE GONNA BE THE NEW DARLING OF "TIME'S" READERSHIP!

RIGHT, ZONK! YOU'LL **BE FAMOUS!** YOU'LL BE NATIONALLY **KNOWN!**

TERRIFIC. A NATIONALLY KNOWN PERVERT..

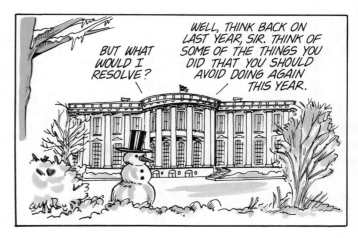

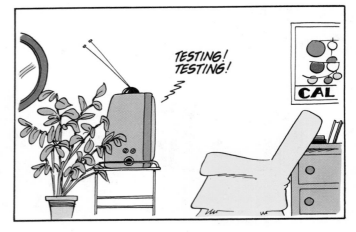

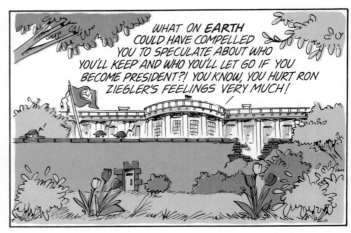

WELL.. I DUNNO, SIR... WITH ALL DUE RESPECT, I THINK WE'RE RUNNING OUT OF PLACES YOU'RE WELCOME TO SPEAK...

WELL, CHECK YOUR LIST AGAIN! IT'S CRUCIAL THAT WE MOVE FORWARD IN BREAKING THE BACK OF MY CREDIBILITY GAP!

WELL.. HERE'S ONE, MR. PRESIDENT— FRITTERS, ALABAMA! POPULATION 1,635. ALL WHITE, 95% OF WORK FORCE WORKING ON GOVERNMENT CONTRACTS!

WHY, IT'S PERFECT, SIR!

"FRITTERS, ALABAMA"?

REPEATING THE TOP STORY. TOMORROW THE PRESIDENT WILL BE FLYING TO FRITTERS, ALABAMA, TO DELIVER A MAJOR SPEECH!

FRITTERS, ALABAMA! CAN YOU BELIEVE IT?! WHAT A JOKE! HA, HA, HEE!

LESS'N, OF COURSE, Y'ALL HAPPIN TO LIVE THERE.

WASHINGTON POST!? WHERE'D YOU GET THAT PAPER, BOY?!

LIBRARY, POP... TEACHER SAYS IF THE PRESIDENT'S COMIN' TO FRITTERS, WE OUGHTA READ UP ON THE BIG PROBLEM HE'S HAVIN' IN WASHINGTON!

HOGWASH, BOY! YOU DON'T NEED A FANCY PAPER LIKE THAT TO KNOW WHAT'S GOIN' ON. DO YOU THINK THE PRESIDENT EVER READS PAPERS LIKE THAT?! YOU KIN BET YOUR BOOTS HE DON'T!

TEACHER SAYS THAT'S PART OF THE PROBLEM.

YOU SASSIN' ME, BOY?!

THERE HE IS, POP!

YUP AND HE'S GETTIN' A MESS OF CHEERS! FOLKS HERE IN FRITTERS BELIEVE IN AMERICA!

POP, YOU MEAN BELIEVIN' IN AMERICA IS THE SAME THANG AS BELIEVIN' IN PRESIDENT NIXON?

OF COURSE! IT STANDS TO REASON, DON'T IT?

HOW YA FIGURE, POP?

SHUT UP AND WAVE YOUR FLAG, BOY!

FOR OBVIOUS REASONS, THERE CAN BE NO PRESENTATION OF THE AWARD FOR BEST FEMALE CONSPIRATOR. THE ABSENCE OF WATERGATE WOMEN IS THE SUBJECT OF MICHAEL DOONESBURY'S ANALYSIS.

BECAUSE OF SEXIST POLICIES IN THE WHITE HOUSE, THERE WERE NO WOMEN IN ON THE DECISION-MAKING PROCESS OF THE COVER-UP. WHILE MS. WOODS AND MS. HARMONY DID THEIR PARTS, THEY WERE NOT IN REAL POSITIONS OF POWER.

WE RECOGNIZE THE PREVAILING BELIEF THAT WOMEN ARE "UNABLE TO KEEP A SECRET," BUT IN OUR JUDGMENT, THIS DOES NOT JUSTIFY WITHHOLDING FROM WOMEN THEIR EQUAL RIGHT TO OBSTRUCT JUSTICE!

WE, THE MANAGEMENT OF WBBY, DEPLORE THIS SITUATION.

WE INVITE YOUR COMMENTS, TOO.

WELL, I'M OFF NOW, JEN. HOLD DOWN THE FORT.

I WILL, CONGRESSMAN. SAY, WHY ARE YOU FLYING HOME NOW, ANYWAY?

I WANT TO TALK TO SOME OF MY CONSTITUENTS, JENNY — TO SEE HOW THEY FEEL ABOUT IMPEACHMENT. I WANT THEM TO KNOW THAT I'M RESPONSIVE TO FOLKS IN MY DISTRICT!

WITH MY OWN ELECTION COMING UP, I ALSO HAVE TO SHOW THEM THAT I'M AN HONEST, CARING PUBLIC SERVANT, THAT I'VE DEVELOPED GREAT POST-WATERGATE MORALS!

OH, CONGRESSMAN, YOU'VE ALWAYS HAD POST-WATERGATE MORALS!

HEE, HEE! SEE YOU, BEAUTIFUL!

SO THAT'S WHY I'M HERE BOYS — IMPEACHMENT! I WANT YOUR VIEWS, YOUR THOUGHTS ON HOW MY VOTE SHOULD GO!

WHATCHA ASKIN' US FER NOW, ED? — YEW ALWAYS VOTED ANY WAY YEW DANG PLEASED BEFORE! YEW DONE VOTED FER THAT FOOL WAR FER EIGHT YEARS WITHOUT ASKIN'!

BUT.. BUT.. YOU WERE FOR THE WAR, WEREN'T YOU?

HELL, NO, ED! WE WAS AGIN IT! NEVER SAW MUCH SENSE IN IT.

OH.. HEY, LOOK, I'M SORRY! I FEEL JUST AWFUL..

FORGIT IT, ED! SET 'N HAVE SOME CIDER..

SO, FRIENDS, THOSE ARE THE ANTICIPATED ARTICLES OF IMPEACHMENT. THE KEY ISSUE SEEMS TO BE HONESTY IN THE EXECUTIVE BRANCH...

SPEAKIN' OF HONESTY, ED, I DON'T SUPPOSE YOU BROUGHT YOUR INCOME TAX RETURNS DOWN WITH YOU..

AS A MATTER OF FACT, I DID, WALT! WHAT KIND OF PUBLIC SERVANT WOULD I BE IF I COULDN'T DOCUMENT MY OWN INTEGRITY?!

ANTICIPATING YOUR INTEREST, I HAD MY SECRETARY MAKE COPIES OF MY RETURNS FOR THE LAST FOUR YEARS..

NOTHIN' PERSONAL, ED..

NOT AT ALL, WALTER!

"MASKED BALL"?

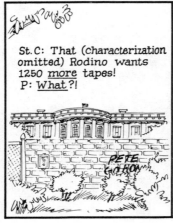

MS. ISABELLE GREBBLE. YOU WERE THE MONEY CZAR'S SECOND-GRADE TEACHER. WHAT CAN YOU TELL US ABOUT HIM?

WELL, I'LL NEVER FORGET HOW MUCH THE LITTLE TYKE USED TO LOVE MONEY! RIGHT FROM THE DAY HE SET UP HIS FIRST BUSINESS, A LEMONADE STAND!

HEE, HEE! I REMEMBER THE LEMONADE USED TO COST HIM 25¢... ONE DAY, AFTER THREE HOURS OF SELLING, HE CAME RUNNING IN WITH 12¢ AND YELLED, "LOOK, MISS GREBBLE, I MADE A NET PROFIT OF 85%!"

HE WAS WRONG, OF COURSE, BUT IT WAS SO ADORABLE!

THE COLLEGE YEARS. THE UBIQUITOUS CZAR-TO-BE WAS A STANDOUT! AN ECONOMICS MAJOR, CLASS TREASURER, AND RESPECTED FRATERNITY MAN.

HIS COLLEGE SWEETHEART, LAURA, NOW MRS. EDDIE BAJOLSKI, REMEMBERS...

THE CZAR REALLY WAS THE MOST MARVELOUS MAN...

HE ALWAYS LOOKED LIKE A MILLION DOLLARS, HE DRESSED TO KILL, AND HE COULD DANCE LIKE ASTAIRE. I ALMOST MARRIED HIM, BUT THEN I ... I MET EDDIE.

I'VE NEVER LOOKED BACK.

HEE, HEE!

WALL STREET. NEW YORK'S YELLOW BRICK ROAD. THE PLACE WHERE A THOUSAND DREAMS ARE REALIZED OR SHATTERED. IT WAS HERE THE YOUNG CZAR FIRST CAME TO SEEK HIS FORTUNE.

BROKERS, INDUSTRIALISTS, BANKERS, MONEY MAGNATES OF ALL KINDS — THESE ARE BILL SIMON'S PEOPLE. THESE ARE THE PEOPLE WHO WATCHED AS HE COOLLY WENT ABOUT MAKING HIS FIRST MILLION.

ALBIE ROBERTS, A FELLOW BROKER IN THE CZAR'S OLD FIRM.

THE GUY WAS A BUM. HE'D SELL HIS OWN CHILDREN IF THE MARKET WERE RIGHT.

YES, IT'S A TOUGH SCENE, WALL STREET..

HOW LONG BILL SIMON PLANS TO STAY ON AT TREASURY IS ANYONE'S GUESS. BUT IN THE MEANTIME, WASHINGTON HAS A NEW STAR.

CZAR. THE MAN AND THE MONEY.

I'M JOHN CHANCELLOR. GOOD NIGHT.

WOOF!

HONEY, HOW COME SHE ISN'T GETTING ALPO?!

V/Brightening Up Our Tarnished Age

The crises break and the walls come down. Not only are the gates working again at the White House, but for this President even poolside isn't too chummy a milieu for meeting the press. And out at Berkeley, the new chumminess gets to Joanie, too, as she finds that having a right-on, law school roommate like Virginia means contending as well with her boyfriend, an improbable homebody named Clyde. If not all of the nation's wounds are healing—witness the lunchroom melee instigated by an eight-year-old participant of forced busing—things do seem to have settled down. And yet . . . Suppose we could get back to when it all started, or even imagine ourselves at Scot Sloan's publication party—with his cat Kent State, with the university president who remembers how it was, with all the gang playing their "best and brightest" roles. Have we come a long enough way to make sport of it all? Or should we wonder, with Mark and Mike, what happened to us?

'COURSE SOME FOLKS, LIKE SWEET VIRGINIA, SEE AN 8-TRACK TAPE DECK AS A LUXURY! BUT IT AIN'T! IT'S A NECESSITY!

IT'S VERY NICE, CLYDE..

'N I GOT THE SILVER FOX FUR SEATS 'CAUSE I'M REALLY INTO COMFORT, SEE?

RIGHT. COMFORT'S PRETTY HIGH ON MY LIST, TOO!

OOH, YASS! THIS HERE'S A FINE MACHINE, AIN'T THAT RIGHT, SWEETHEART?

CAN YA DIG THE CHROME STALLION ON THE HOOD?

OH, YES.. VERY SNAPPY!

CHIP! CHIP!

CHIP! CHIP!

CRUNCH!

GOOD MORNING! FOR THOSE OF YOU REPORTERS WHO ARE NEW HERE, I'M JERRY terHORST, PRESIDENT FORD'S PRESS SECRETARY.

AS MR. FORD'S PRINCIPAL SPOKESMAN, MY ONE WISH IS TO LET YOU KNOW PRECISELY WHAT IS GOING ON, TO PROVIDE YOU WITH A WINDOW INTO THE FORD ADMINISTRATION!

SO IF THERE'S ANYTHING I CAN DO FOR YOU, ANYTHING AT ALL..

JERRY, HOW ABOUT CHANGING YOUR NAME? IT LOOKS LIKE A TYPOGRAPHICAL ERROR.

I'D BE HAPPY TO. ANY SUGGESTIONS?

"SMITH"!

"KOJAK"!

"TRIGGER"!

MR. PRESIDENT, THE WORKMEN HAVE FINISHED RECONVERTING THE PRESS ROOM BACK INTO A POOL..

OH, GOOD, GOOD! LET'S TRY IT OUT!

LADIES AND GENTLEMEN— THE PRESIDENT OF THE UNITED STATES!

SPLASH!

MR. PRESIDENT, MR. PRESIDENT!

WOW! DIDJA SEE THAT GAINER?!

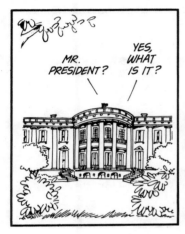

MR. WOOTEN, AFTER FIVE YEARS IN QUEBEC, HOW DO YOU FEEL THE CANADIAN GOVERNMENT COMPARES TO OURS?

NO COMPARISON, MAN! I MEAN, LIKE, CANADIAN GOVERNMENT *WORKS!* THEY JUST KNOW HOW TO DO IT *RIGHT!*

YEAH! TAKE CAMPUS DISORDERS, FOR EXAMPLE! IN THE U.S., THE PRESIDENT TRIED TO DEAL WITH THE PROBLEM OF STUDENT UNREST WITH LOTS OF *RIOT POLICE* — YOU KNOW, THE WHOLE *REPRESSION* TRIP!

BUT DO YOU KNOW WHAT THE PRIME MINISTER OF CANADA DID WHEN FACED WITH THE SAME PROBLEM? DO YOU?

HE MARRIED A CO-ED!

NOW *THAT'S* CLASS, MAN!

THAT'S THE END OF THE CONFERENCE, GUYS! WE GOTTA GET BACK TO *CANADA!* BACK TO THE TALL, WHISPERIN' PINES, 'N HOT MAPLE SYRUP..

..RED COATED MOUNTIES PERCHED HIGH IN THEIR STIRRUPS..

..HARD, RUBBER HOCKEY PUCKS SHOT FROM THE WING..

..THESE ARE A FEW OF OUR *FAAVORITE* THINGS!!

HEE! HA! HA! HA, HA! HEE! HEE!

WE ALSO DIG THE QUEEN..

GOD SAVE HER! SHE KEPT OUR BOYS OUT OF *CHILE!*

C'MON, RALPHIE, JUST ONE VERSE!

ZONKER! YOUR PLANTS HAVE SECRET LIVES?

NO SECRET ABOUT IT, MICHAEL — PLANTS ARE VERY ARTICULATE! IF YOU LISTEN REAL CLOSELY, YOU MIGHT BE ABLE TO HEAR ED THE GERANIUM RECITE "GUNGA DIN"!

DID HE SAY ANYTHING YET?

NOPE. MUST BE ASLEEP.

THE KEY THING IS HUMIDITY! SEE, IF YOU..

"YOU'RE A BETTER MAN THAN I, SENOR DIN!" ALAS, POOR GUNGA, I KNEW HIM WELL!

HEE! HEE!

HEY, C'MON, PIPE DOWN!! I'M TRYING TO TALK TO MIKE!

SEE, IF YOU..

IS THAT A NEW SHOOT I SEE THERE?

OH, ED, YOU NOTICED!

TORTS?.. NO, I DON'T WANT TO TALK ABOUT TORTS! WE JUST SPENT ALL MORNING TALKING ABOUT TORTS!

WOODROW, WHAT YOU'VE GOT TO REALIZE IS THAT THE WORLD DOESN'T BEGIN AND END WITH CASEBOOKS! THERE ARE MANY OTHER EQUALLY ACCEPTABLE WAYS OF LOOKING AT LIFE!

HMM..

YEAH, I SUPPOSE YOU COULD MAKE A CASE FOR THAT..

WELL, REALLY NOW, WOODROW, IT'S ONLY A MATTER OF CIVIL PRO- CEDURE!

TRUE—BUT ONLY AS FAR AS IT AFFECTS THE INCLUSION OF PARTIES NECES- SARY FOR THE DISPOSITION!

HEY, PEOPLE! I'VE GOT A REALLY CRAZY, FAR-OUT, ZANY IDEA! LET'S SPEND PART OF LUNCH TALKING ABOUT SOMETHING OTHER THAN LAW!

FORGIVE ME. I LOST MY HEAD.

WHO IS THIS CHICK?

JOAN SOME- BODY.

Dear Mr. President,

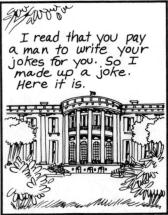

I read that you pay a man to write your jokes for you. So I made up a joke. Here it is.

You say, "I am a Ford, not a Lincoln, and Ford has a better idea."

Please pay me $10.00 for this joke. Your friend, Billy R.

WHERE DO YOU THINK YOU'RE GOING, YOUNG MAN?

I'M MOVIN' IN WITH VIRGINIA, POCATELLI.

BANG! BANG!

WELL, AS I UNDERSTAND IT, VIRGINIA DOESN'T WANT YOU TO MOVE IN!

HEY, POCATELLI— YOU GO MIND YOUR OWN BUSINESS, HEAR?

OH, HI, CLYDE— WHAT'S UP?

ZIP!

HELLO?.. GET ME THE BERKELEY POLICE!

UH..CAN I COME IN?.. QUICK?!

DEPENDS, LOVER— WHAT DO WE GOT HERE?

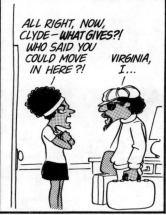

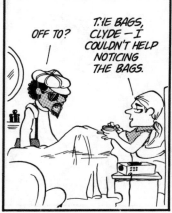

CLYDE, LOOK—HERE'S WHERE I'M AT: I HAPPEN TO LIKE YOU VERY MUCH, AND I PLACE A LOT OF VALUE ON OUR FRIENDSHIP. I ALSO THINK YOU'RE ONE OF THE SEXIER PEOPLE I'VE EVER MET..

BUT, ALL THAT NOTWITHSTANDING, I DON'T WANT TO GET MARRIED, I DON'T WANT TO LIVE WITH ANYONE—I JUST WANT ROOM TO GROW AND BREATHE. CAN'T YOU ACCEPT THAT?

⟨SIGH⟩.. YEAH.. YEAH, I GUESS I CAN DIG IT..

S'LONG AS YOU REALLY MEAN THE SEXY PART!

HEY, C'MON! YOU SLAY ME, LOVER.

McAFEE IS DOWN! HE WAS HIT VERY, VERY HARD! TIME OUT ON THE FIELD!

THE DOCTORS ARE RUSHING OUT ON THE FIELD.. THEY'RE CHECKING HIM OUT... McAFEE'S BEING PUT ON THE STRETCHER!

ROG, WE JUST GOT A REPORT HERE FROM OUR MAN ON THE FIELD! IT SEEMS THAT McAFEE IS...UH.. DEAD.

YES, BUT WHAT A HAND HE'S GETTING THERE, JACK!

RIGHT! I'LL TELL YOU, ROGER—THESE ARE SOME KINDA FOOTBALL FANS!

AS PART OF NBC'S CONTINUING COVERAGE OF THE MARIJUANA CRISIS, TODAY WE INTERVIEW DR. R.G. TULANE, WHO RECENTLY LINKED THE USAGE OF MARIJUANA TO BRAIN DAMAGE!

DOCTOR, WE UNDERSTAND THAT HEAVY EXPOSURE TO MARIJUANA HAS CAUSED SOME INSIDIOUS EFFECTS IN YOUR RHESUS MONKEYS!

THAT IS CORRECT...

MY MONKEYS WERE GIVEN A CONTROLLED DAILY DOSAGE. AFTER ONLY TWO WEEKS, INTENSIVE INTERVIEWS WERE CONDUCTED WITH EACH OF THEM.

AND?..

THEY WERE ALL TOTALLY INCOHERENT.

UH-OH..

HEY, REV—WHAT A NICE SURPRISE! WHAT BRINGS YOU OUT HERE?

ZONKER, IT'S MY NOVEL—IT'S FINALLY BEEN ACCEPTED FOR PUBLICATION!

HEY, THAT'S GREAT, SCOTTY!

THEY SAY THEY LOVE IT! THEY SAY I'M GOING TO BE FAMOUS, A STAR! I'M BEING SENT ON A 30-CITY TOUR—TALK SHOWS, AUTOGRAPH PARTIES, THE WORKS!

THAT'S WHY I CAME OUT HERE, ZONK! I HAD TO GET OUT OF THE CITY, TO GET IN TOUCH WITH MYSELF BEFORE IT ALL BEGINS!

OH... WELL, YOU CAN USE MIKE'S ROOM IF YOU WANT..

THANKS, ZONK. I APPRECIATE IT!

SO WHAT'S THIS NEW BLOCKBUSTER OF YOURS ABOUT, REV?

WELL, IT TRACES THE GROWTH OF A YOUNG PHILOSOPHY STUDENT WHO GETS INVOLVED IN THE BERKELEY FREE-SPEECH MOVEMENT, THEN MOVES ON TO A BUDDHIST COMMUNE IN MICHIGAN..

MORE! MORE!

LATER, HE IS ARRESTED FOR CONSPIRACY IN CHICAGO, BUT ESCAPES TO BECOME A MEDIC AT WOODSTOCK. FINALLY, FREAKED OUT OVER THE WAR, AND WIRED ON SIX TABS OF ACID, HE DRIVES HIS V.W. CAMPER OVER A CLIFF AT MALIBU!

IT'S SORT OF ABOUT THE SIXTIES.

YEAH, MAN, I BEEN THERE..

MICHAEL! DID YOU HEAR ABOUT THE GOOD REVEREND'S NOVEL?!

YOU BET! I JUST SAW HIM THIS MORNING. HE DROPPED BY WALDEN WITH A PHOTOGRAPHER!

WITH A PHOTOGRAPHER? WHAT FOR?

HE WANTS TO BORROW OUR SCENERY FOR A BACK JACKET PHOTO..

HOW'S THIS?

‹CLICK!› GOOD! ‹CLICK› GOOD! OKAY, NOW LET'S SEE SOME TEETH!

WHATCHA DOING NOW, W.S.?

WRITING MY BIO. FOR THE JACKET FLAP...

TAP! TAP! TAP!

W.S. Sloan, Jr., is a dedicated activist of long standing. He was once described by "Look" magazine as "the fighting young priest who makes a difference."

TAP! TAP! TAP!

Mr. Sloan resides in New England. He lives alone with his faithful Irish setter, Unconditional Amnesty.

TAP! TAP! TAP!

DON'T FORGET OL' KENT STATE..

..and his cat, Kent State.

TAP! TAP! TAP!

ZONKER! YOU'RE ALL DRESSED UP!

YUP! I'M OFF TO SCOT'S PUBLICATION PARTY! HE'S HAVING A SORT OF SIXTIES REVIVAL COSTUME BALL!

SIXTIES REVIVAL?

YOU KNOW—STROBE LIGHTS, OPPRESSIVELY LOUD MUSIC, LOTS OF PSYCHEDELICS—THAT SORT OF THING!

SOUNDS LIKE FUN! WHAT'S THAT YOU GOT ON—SORT OF GYPSY GARB?

NOPE. IT'S MY SICK, TWISTED, NEO-FASCIST DRUG-FIEND DISGUISE.

OH. WELL, YOU LOOK JUST GREAT!

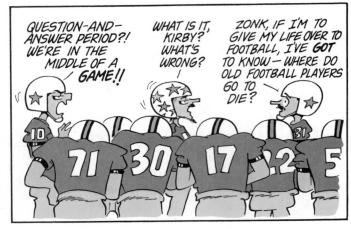

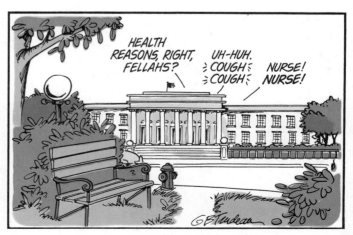

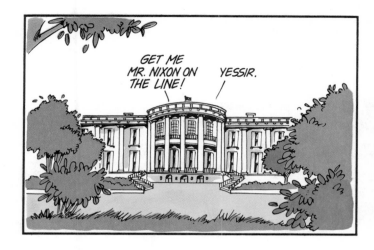

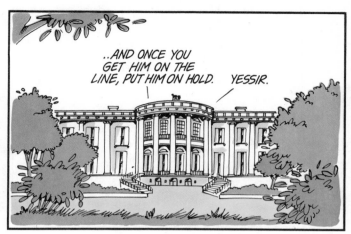

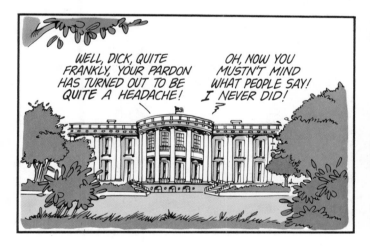

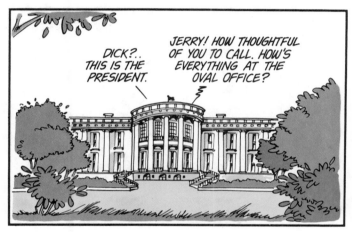

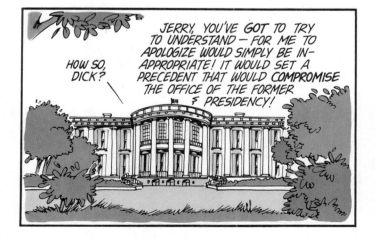